A WHO HQ GRAPHIC NOVEL

What Made California the Golden State?

LIFE DURING T

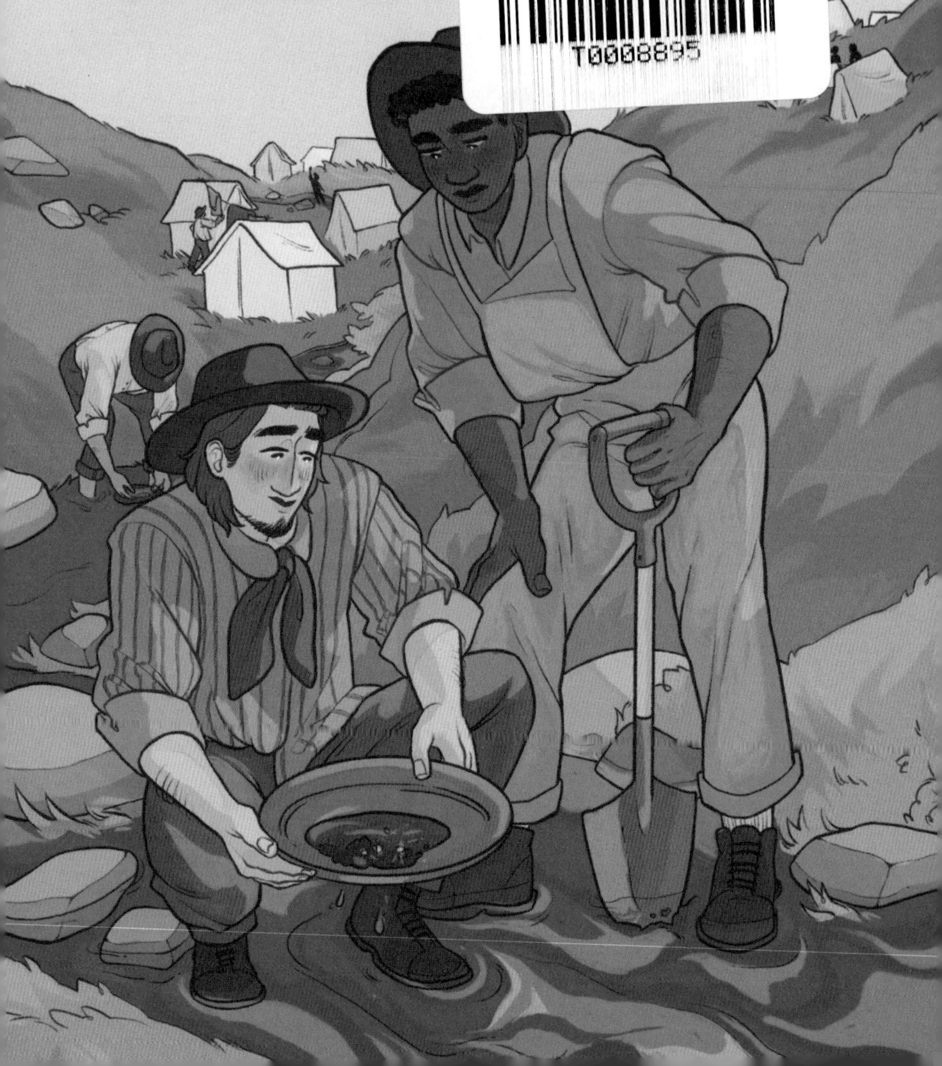

For everyone who didn't see themselves in history,
and so looked harder—SYK

To everyone who supported this book along the way—
and to the real William and Henry, whose story lived on
outside of these pages. I hope you lived well, and don't mind
how I've drawn you—KG

PENGUIN WORKSHOP
An imprint of Penguin Random House LLC, New York

First published in the United States of America by Penguin Workshop,
an imprint of Penguin Random House LLC, New York, 2024

Visit us online at penguinrandomhouse.com.

Library of Congress Cataloging-in-Publication Data is available.

Manufactured in China

ISBN 9780593385869 (pbk)   10 9 8 7 6 5 4 3 2 1 HH
ISBN 9780593385852 (hc)   10 9 8 7 6 5 4 3 2 1 HH

Lettering by Comicraft
Design by Jay Emmanuel

This is a work of nonfiction. All of the events that unfold in the narrative
are rooted in historical fact. Some dialogue and characters have been fictionalized
in order to illustrate or teach a historical point.

For more information about your favorite historical figures, places, and events,
please visit whohq.com.

A WHO HQ GRAPHIC NOVEL

What Made California the Golden State?

LIFE DURING THE GOLD RUSH

by Shing Yin Khor
illustrated by Kass Gray

Penguin Workshop

Introduction

On January 24, 1848, American sawmill operator James Marshall found gold near his employer John Sutter's mill, just nine days before America would take California from Mexico at the end of the Mexican-American War. This was the event that sparked what is known as the California Gold Rush, a period in which hundreds of thousands of people moved to California seeking their own fortunes. The problem was that neither James Marshall nor John Sutter would actually become rich. Instead, Samuel Brannan, a newspaper publisher and businessman who first publicized the gold find, became the Gold Rush's first millionaire by selling equipment to miners at hugely inflated prices.

By 1849, California saw approximately ninety thousand people from all over the world arriving to seek riches with nothing more than gold pans, spades, and dreams: Chinese immigrants who called California *Gum San* 金山, or Gold Mountain; enslaved Black people who negotiated their freedom in exchange for labor; Mexicans from mining districts farther south; and Americans from eastern states who crossed the Appalachian Mountains and traveled down rivers to form wagon trains headed westward.

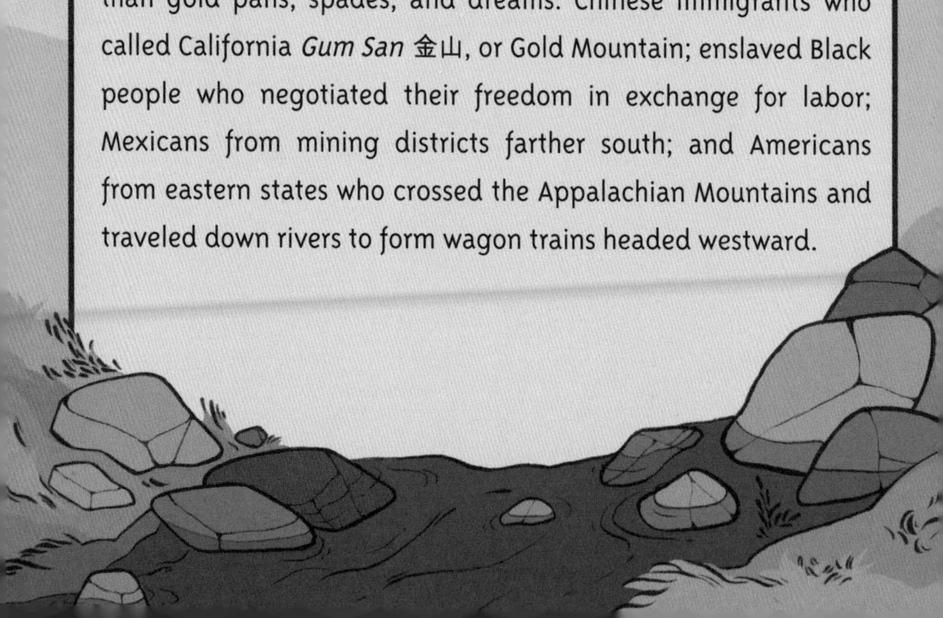

Indigenous people of the region, such as the Plains and Sierra Miwok, mined for gold, too, but they were quickly forced out or killed by the thousands of new arrivals in California.

Life in the goldfields was difficult. Those that did strike gold found themselves faced with high prices for ordinary supplies like mining pans, shovels, and work clothing. There was hard work, and long, hopeless days, but there was also camaraderie and community. Men shared their work, food, and stories for both survival and comfort. For instance, in the Southern Mines (an area in Northern California near the Sierra Nevada mountain range that now includes Tuolumne County and Yosemite National Park), there were two neighboring mining camps of white men and free Black men. There, William Miller and Henry Garrison, a white man and a Black man, cooked and mined together—all in the hopes of one day striking gold.

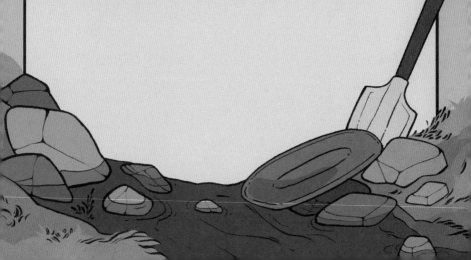

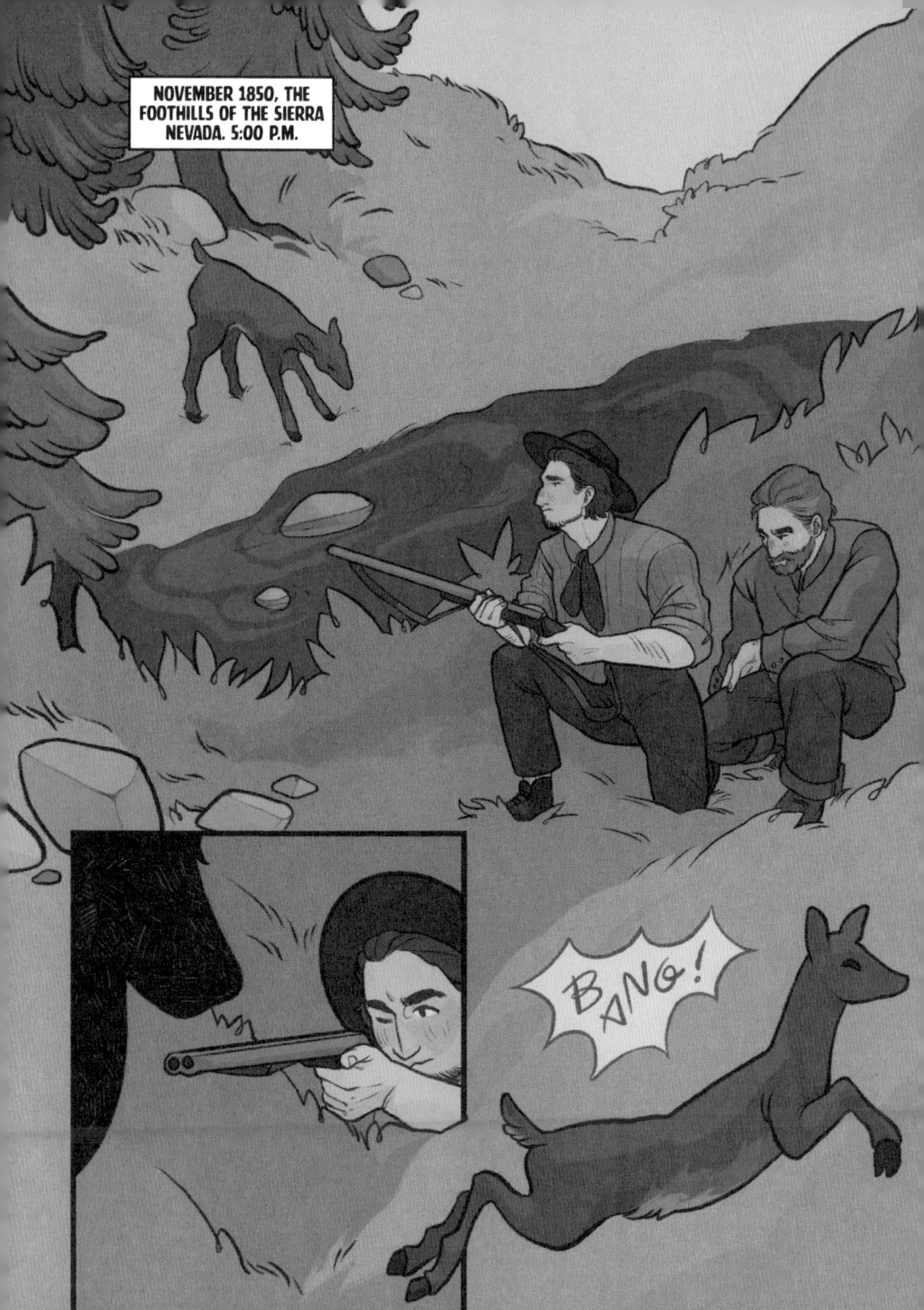
NOVEMBER 1850, THE FOOTHILLS OF THE SIERRA NEVADA. 5:00 P.M.
BANG!

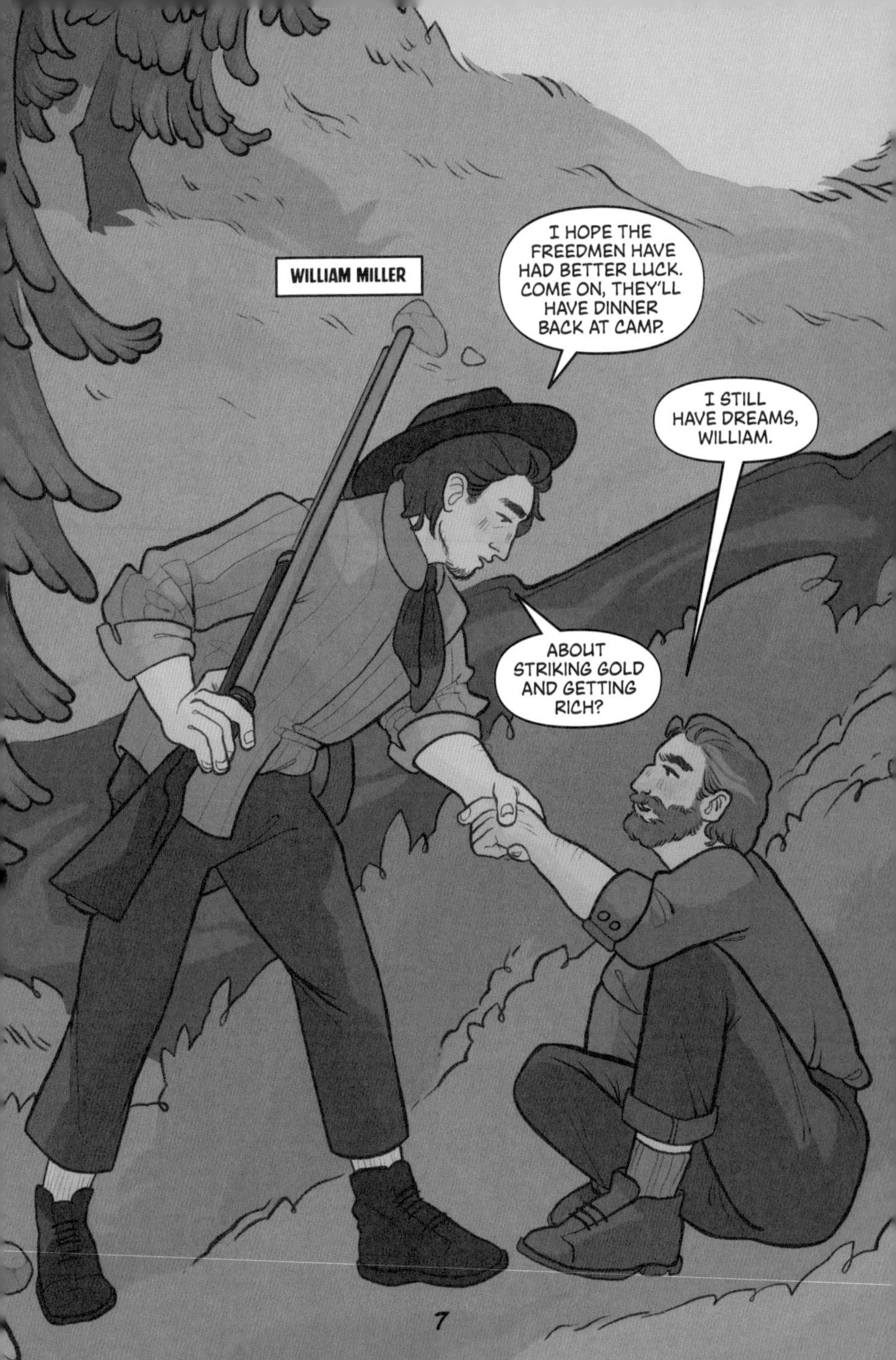
WILLIAM MILLER
I HOPE THE FREEDMEN HAVE HAD BETTER LUCK. COME ON, THEY'LL HAVE DINNER BACK AT CAMP.
I STILL HAVE DREAMS, WILLIAM.
ABOUT STRIKING GOLD AND GETTING RICH?

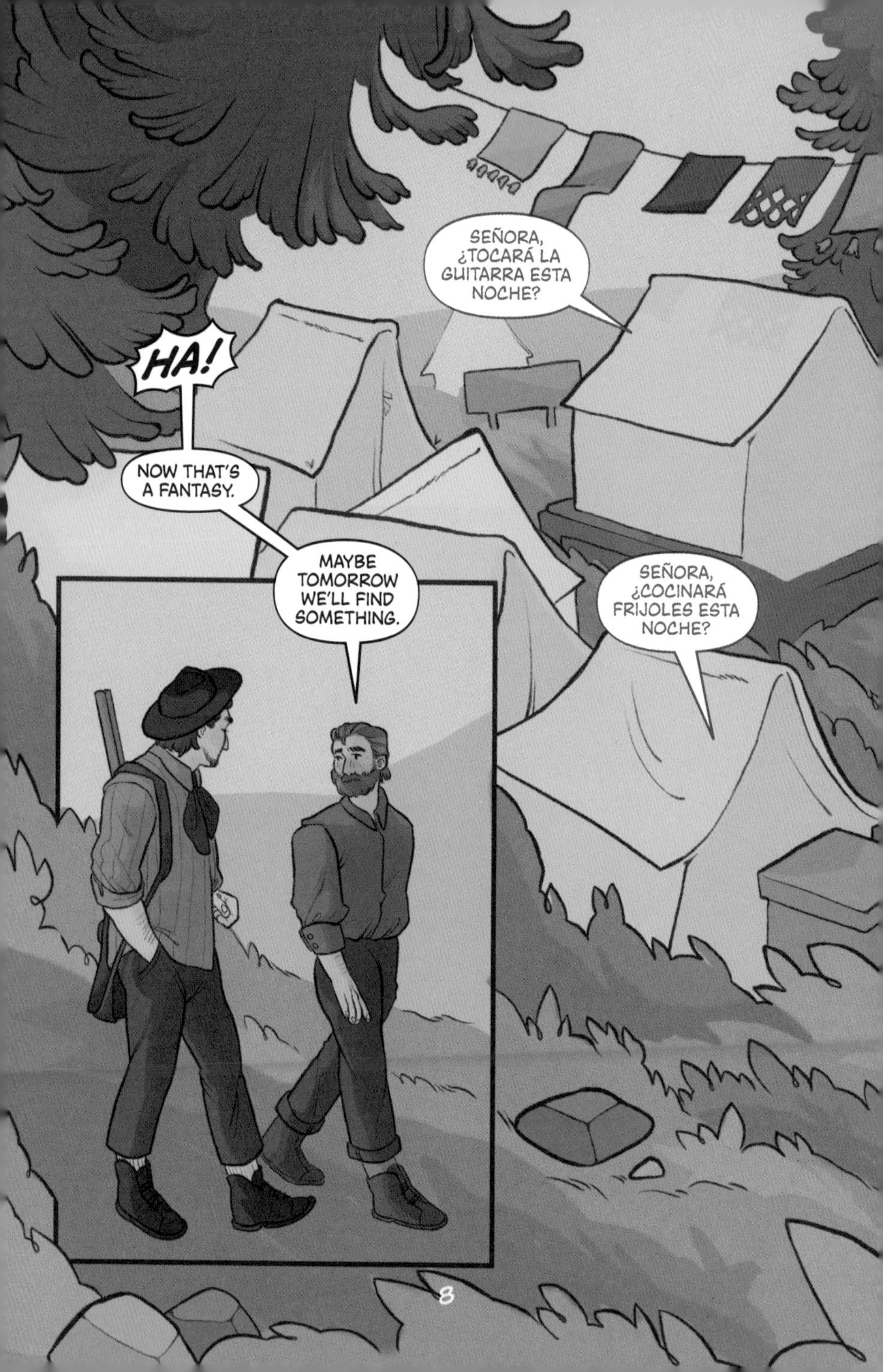
SEÑORA, ¿TOCARÁ LA GUITARRA ESTA NOCHE?
HA!
NOW THAT'S A FANTASY.
SEÑORA, ¿COCINARÁ FRIJOLES ESTA NOCHE?
MAYBE TOMORROW WE'LL FIND SOMETHING.

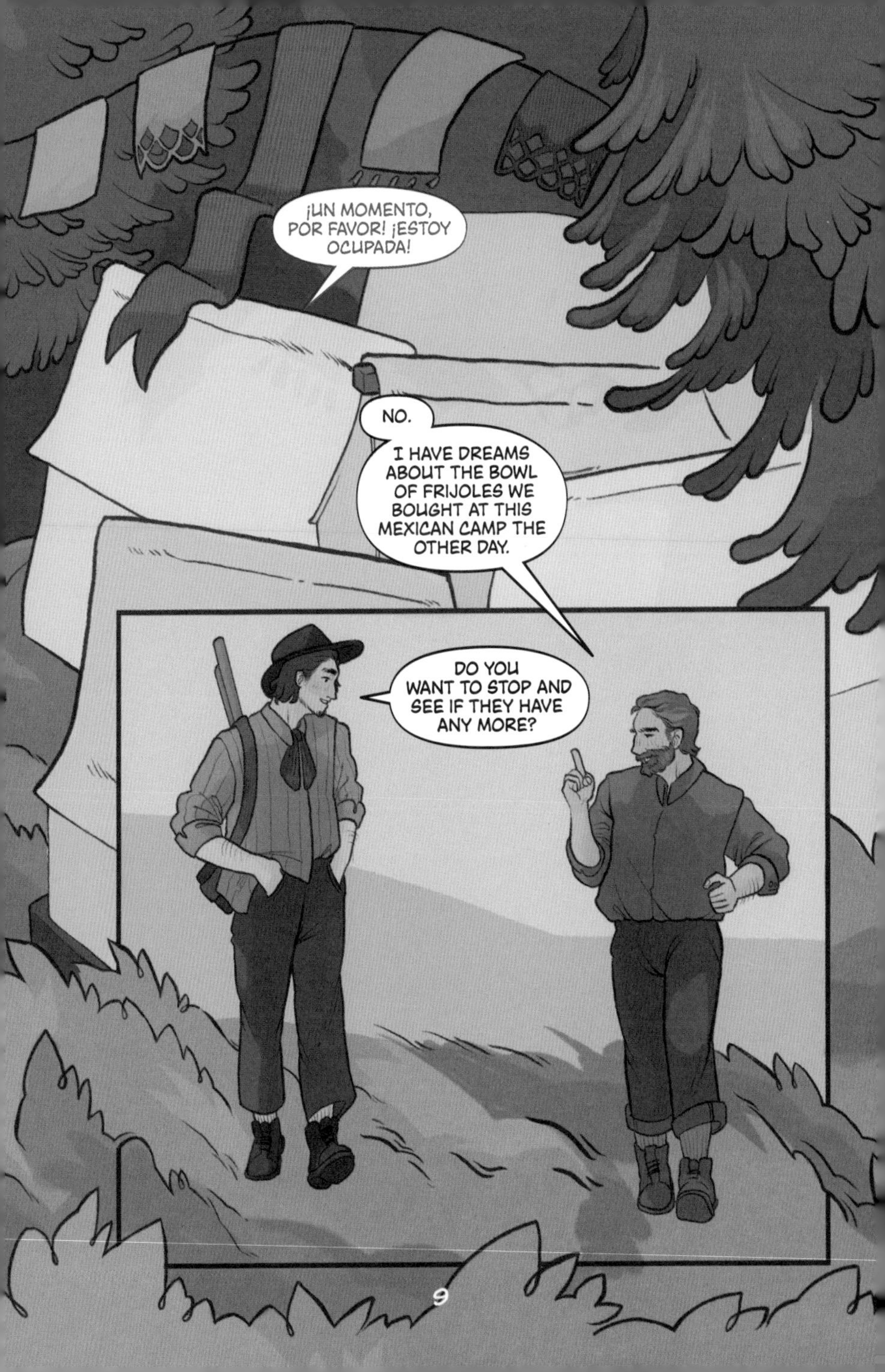
¡UN MOMENTO, POR FAVOR! ¡ESTOY OCUPADA!
NO.
I HAVE DREAMS ABOUT THE BOWL OF FRIJOLES WE BOUGHT AT THIS MEXICAN CAMP THE OTHER DAY.
DO YOU WANT TO STOP AND SEE IF THEY HAVE ANY MORE?

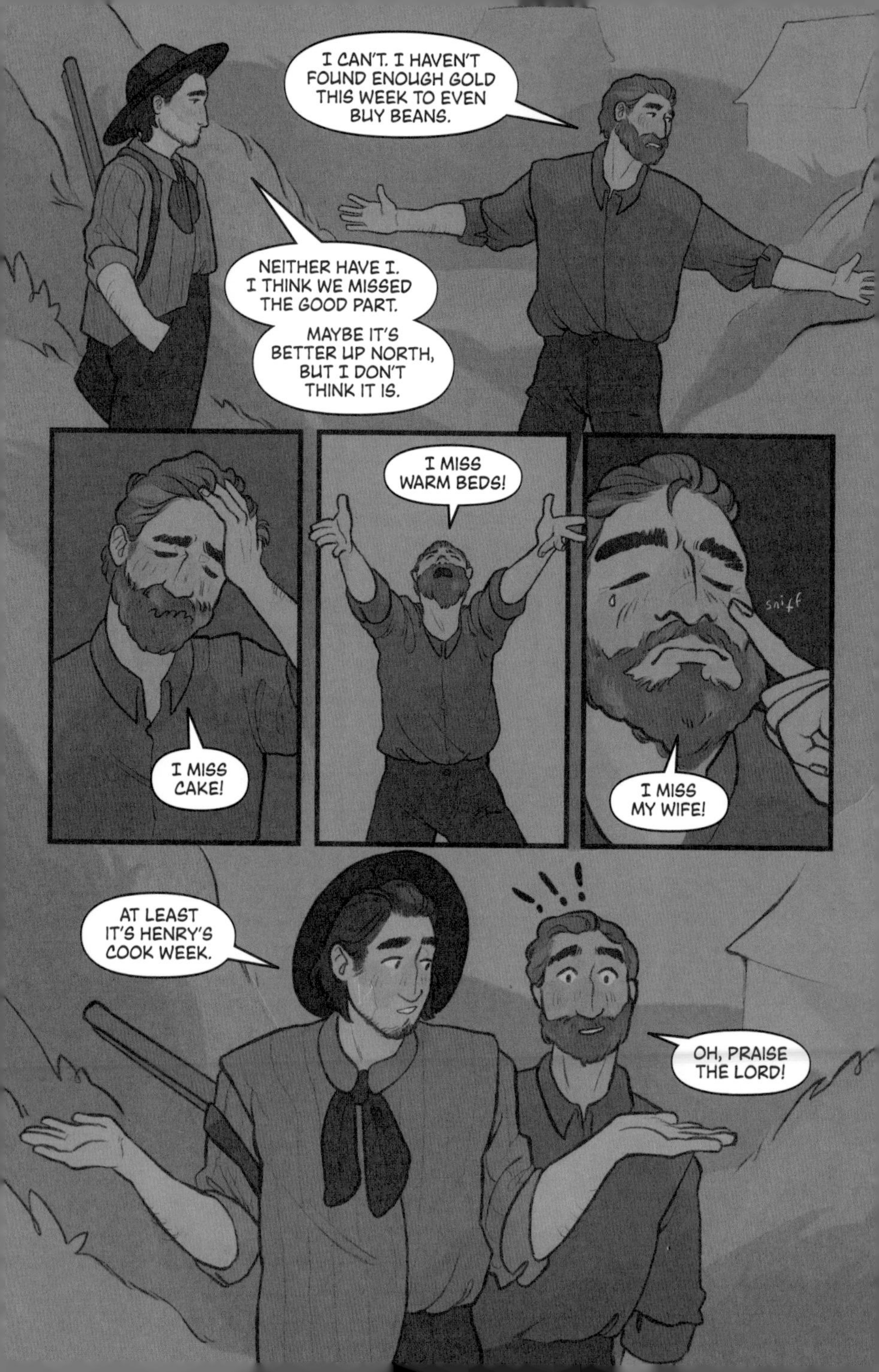
I CAN'T. I HAVEN'T FOUND ENOUGH GOLD THIS WEEK TO EVEN BUY BEANS.
NEITHER HAVE I. I THINK WE MISSED THE GOOD PART.
MAYBE IT'S BETTER UP NORTH, BUT I DON'T THINK IT IS.
I MISS CAKE!
I MISS WARM BEDS!
sniff
I MISS MY WIFE!
AT LEAST IT'S HENRY'S COOK WEEK.
OH, PRAISE THE LORD!

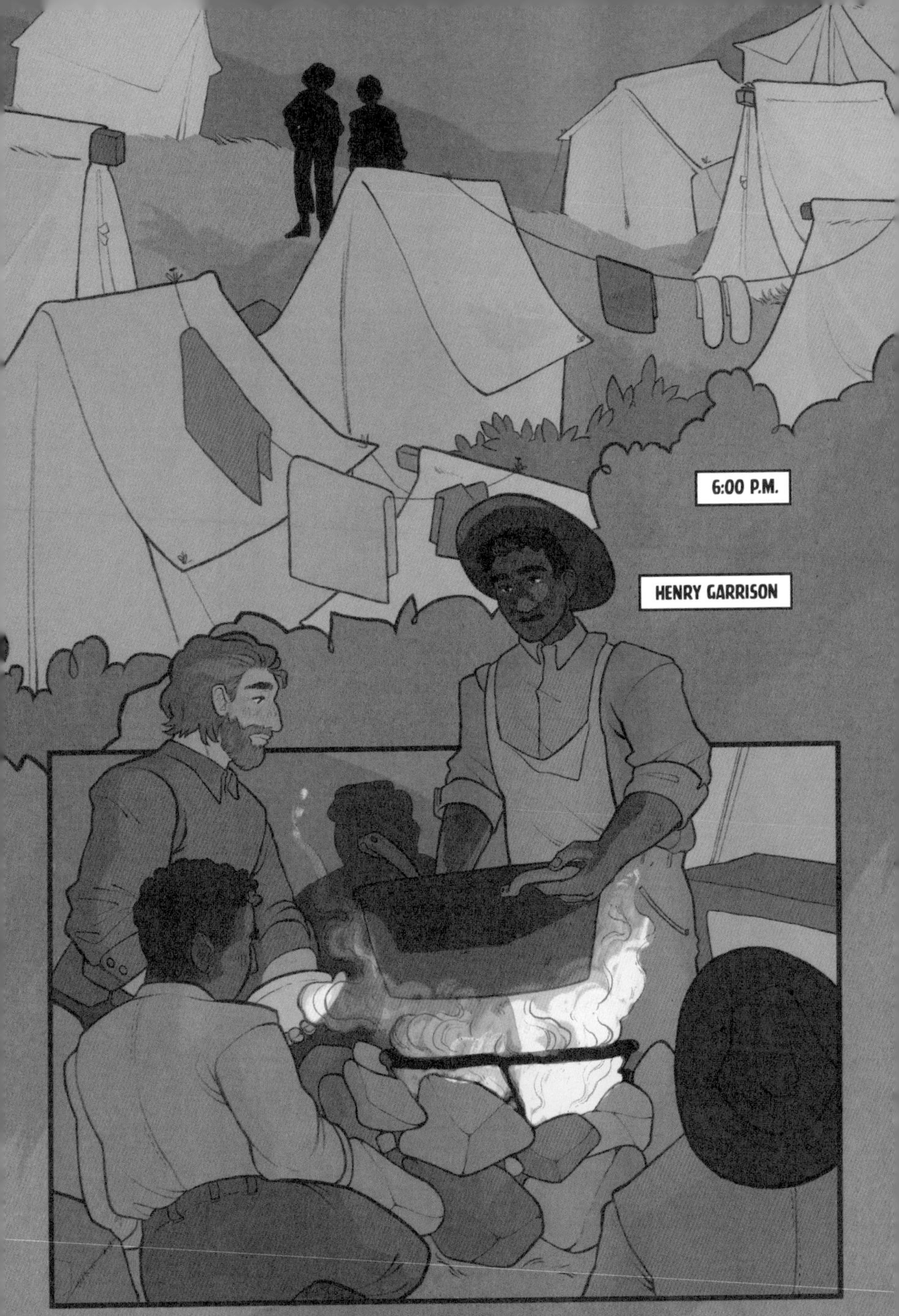
6:00 P.M.
HENRY GARRISON

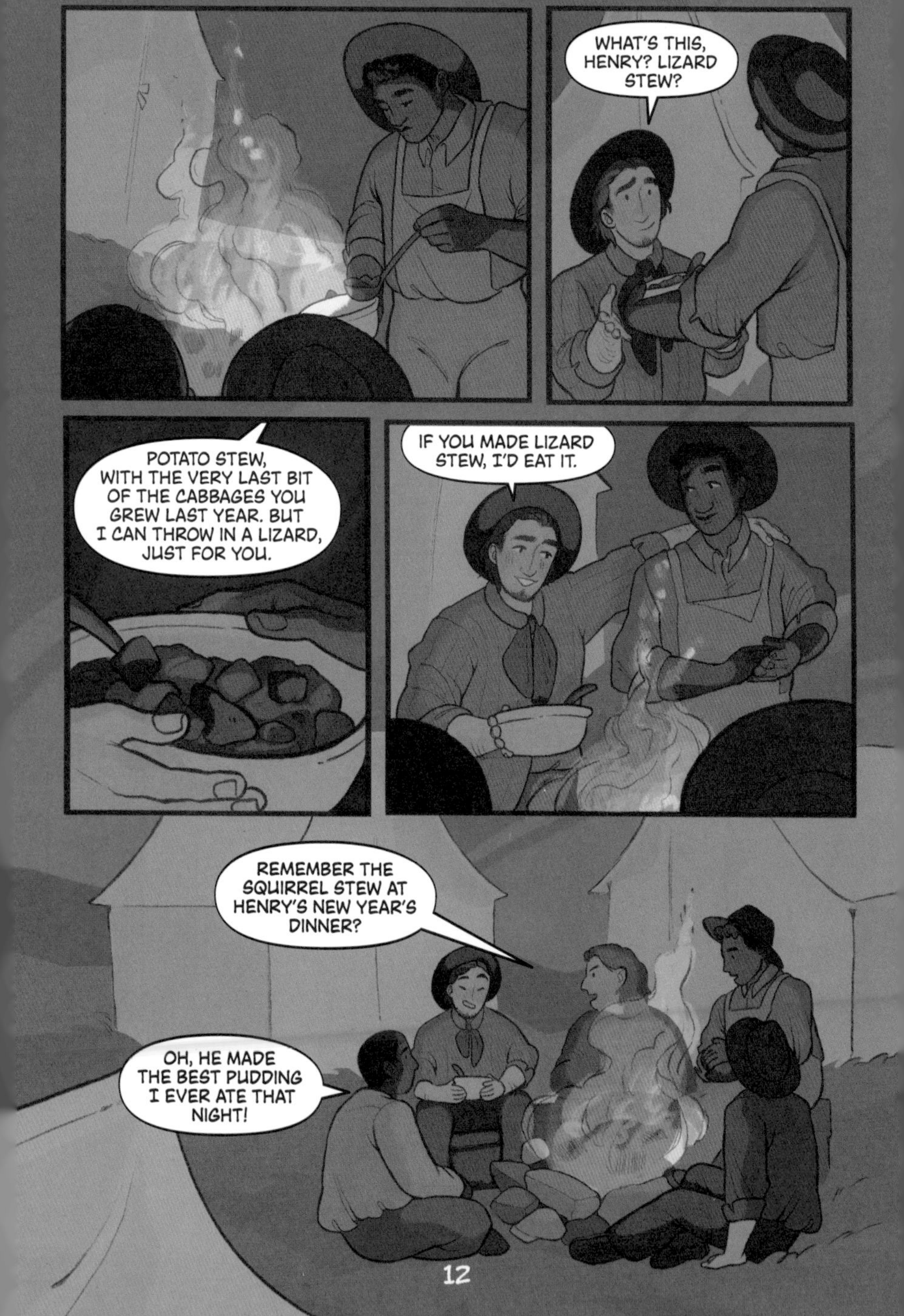
WHAT'S THIS, HENRY? LIZARD STEW?
POTATO STEW, WITH THE VERY LAST BIT OF THE CABBAGES YOU GREW LAST YEAR. BUT I CAN THROW IN A LIZARD, JUST FOR YOU.
IF YOU MADE LIZARD STEW, I'D EAT IT.
REMEMBER THE SQUIRREL STEW AT HENRY'S NEW YEAR'S DINNER?
OH, HE MADE THE BEST PUDDING I EVER ATE THAT NIGHT!

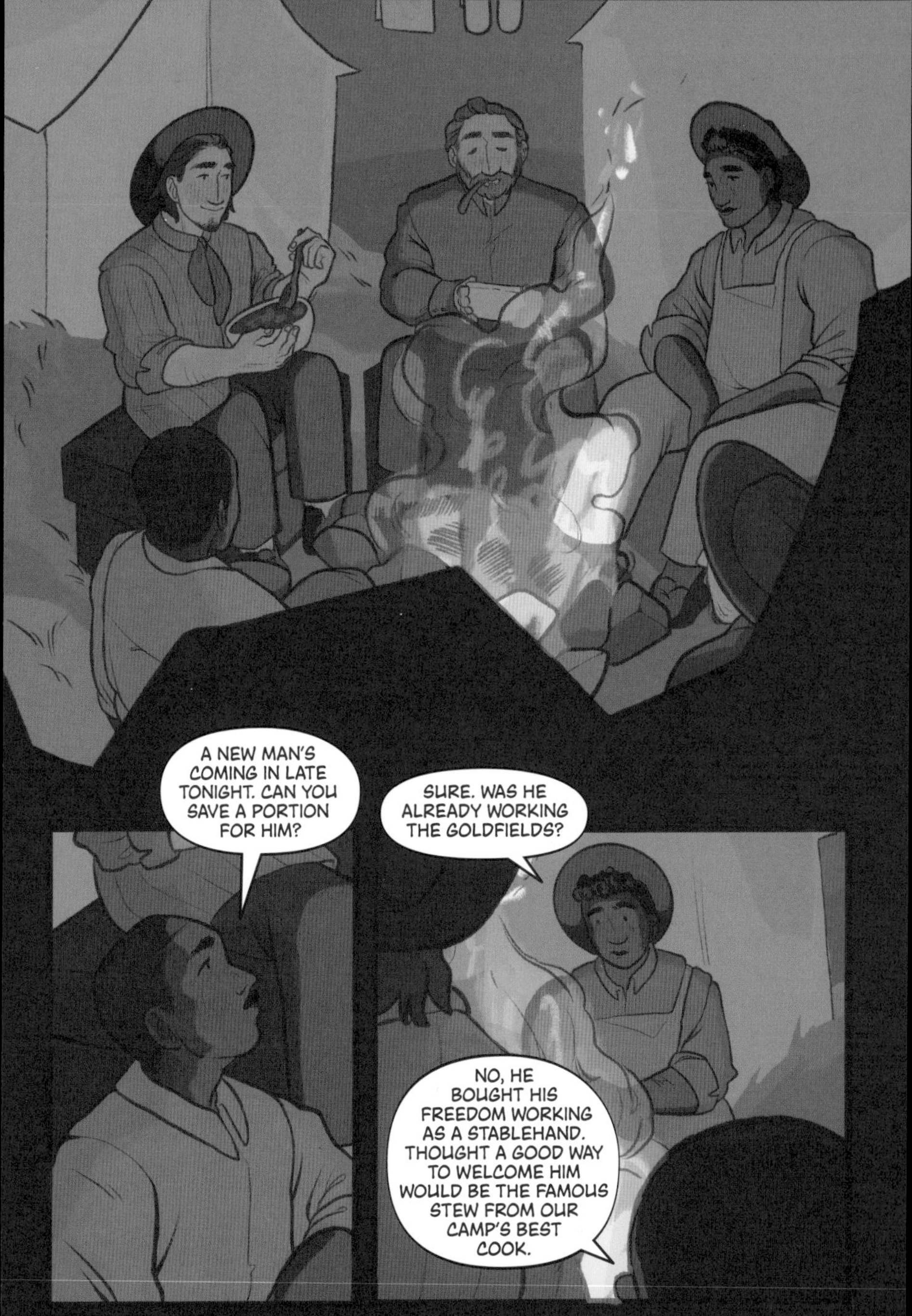
A NEW MAN'S COMING IN LATE TONIGHT. CAN YOU SAVE A PORTION FOR HIM?
SURE. WAS HE ALREADY WORKING THE GOLDFIELDS?
NO, HE BOUGHT HIS FREEDOM WORKING AS A STABLEHAND. THOUGHT A GOOD WAY TO WELCOME HIM WOULD BE THE FAMOUS STEW FROM OUR CAMP'S BEST COOK.

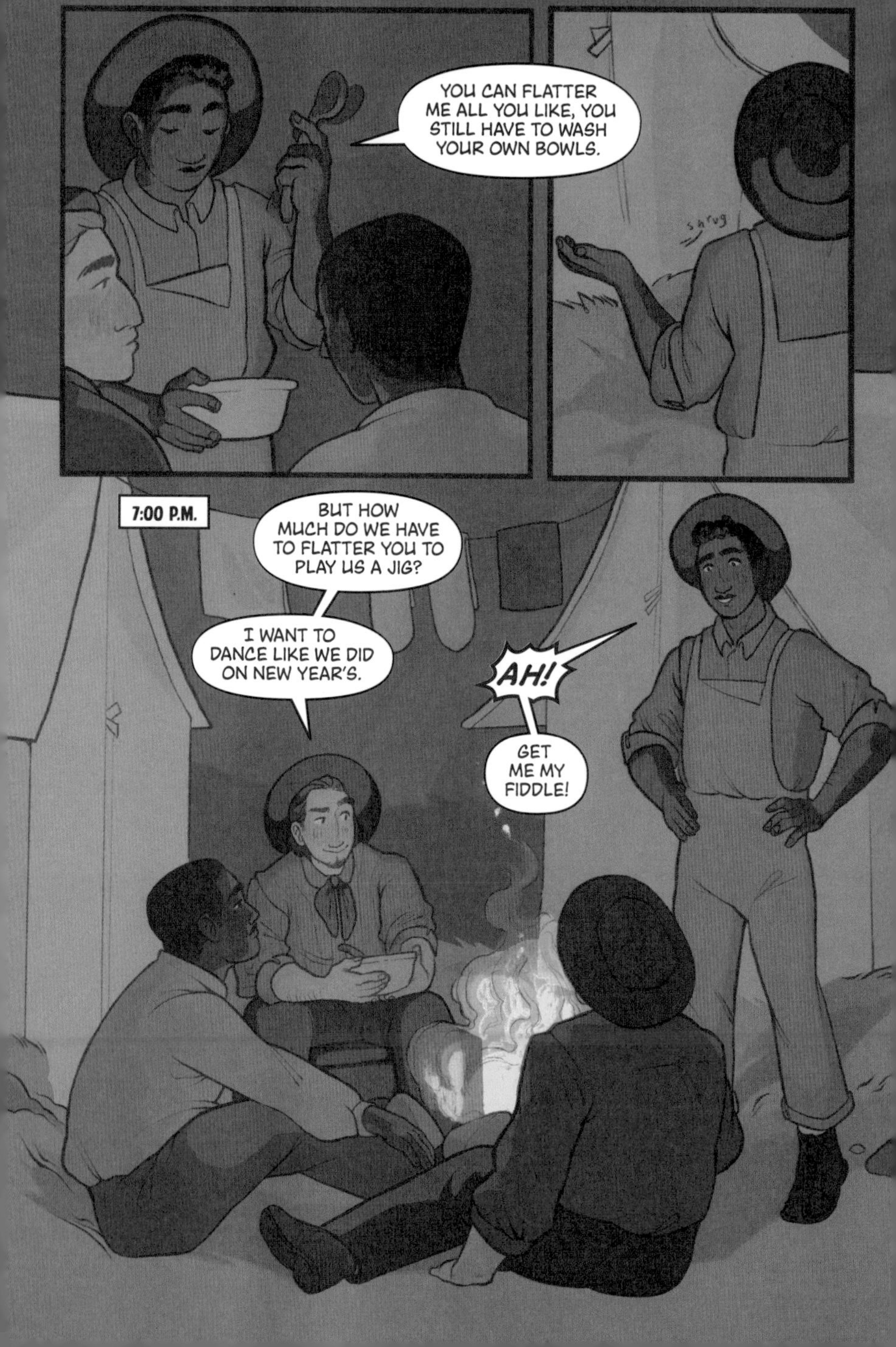
YOU CAN FLATTER ME ALL YOU LIKE, YOU STILL HAVE TO WASH YOUR OWN BOWLS.
shrug
7:00 P.M.
BUT HOW MUCH DO WE HAVE TO FLATTER YOU TO PLAY US A JIG?
I WANT TO DANCE LIKE WE DID ON NEW YEAR'S.
AH!
GET ME MY FIDDLE!

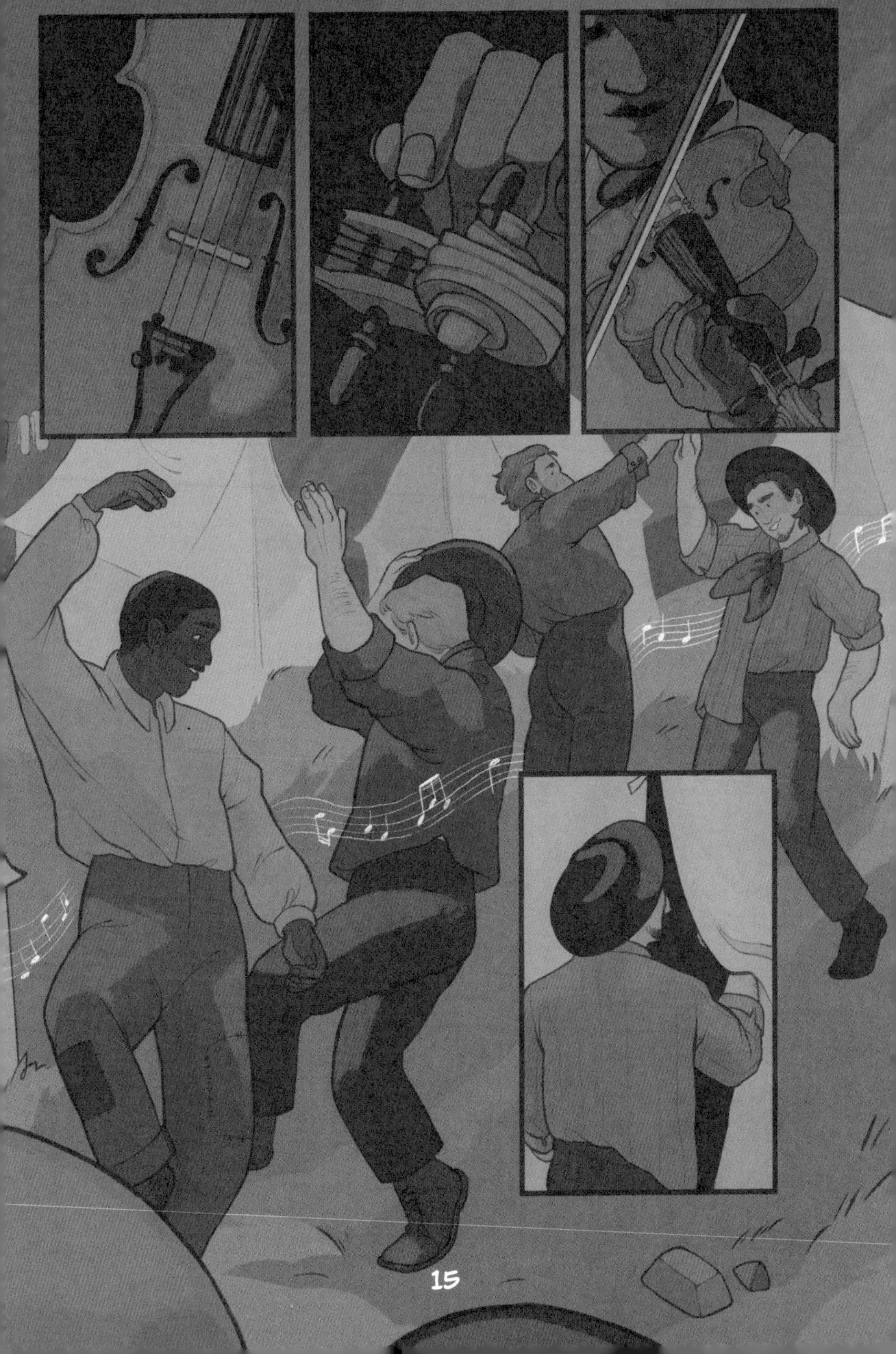

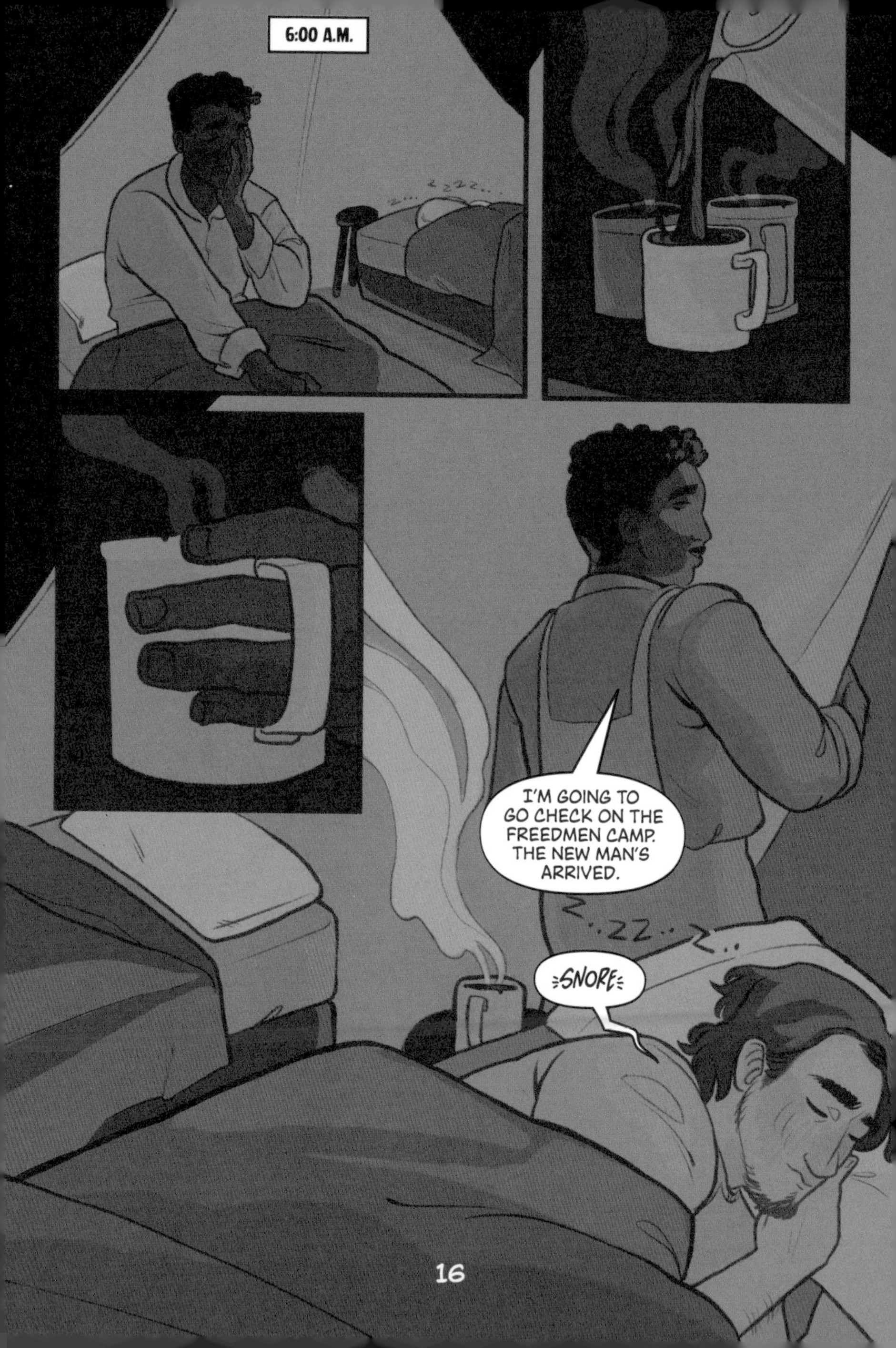
6:00 A.M.
Z..Z.Z..
I'M GOING TO GO CHECK ON THE FREEDMEN CAMP. THE NEW MAN'S ARRIVED.
Z..ZZ..Z..
SNORE

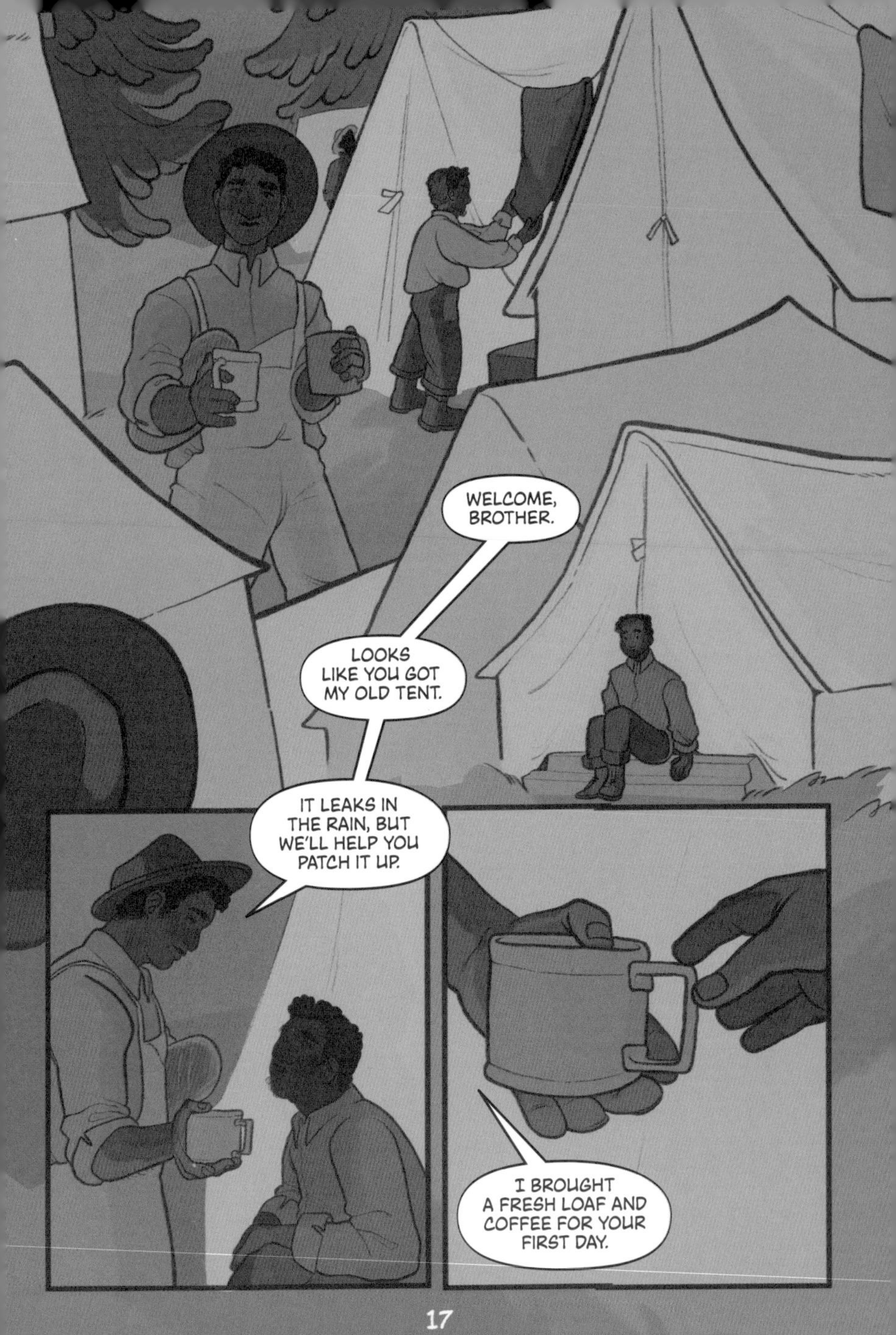
WELCOME, BROTHER.
LOOKS LIKE YOU GOT MY OLD TENT.
IT LEAKS IN THE RAIN, BUT WE'LL HELP YOU PATCH IT UP.
I BROUGHT A FRESH LOAF AND COFFEE FOR YOUR FIRST DAY.

Black Slavery and the Gold Rush

In the early days of the California Gold Rush, slaveholders from Southern states brought enslaved people west to mine and work for them. There were free Black people in the region, and California was trying to join the Union as a free state, so many enslaved people used this opportunity to escape or purchase their freedom with work agreements.

In September 1850, Congress voted to admit California to the Union as a free state, which meant that slavery was technically illegal. However, unlawful slavery was common, and Black people still did not have the right to vote or to testify in court.

In 1852, California passed the Fugitive Slave Law, which said that any enslaved person who had entered California before statehood remained the property of the person who brought them there. Some freed Black men, who had started new lives in California, were arrested and deported. Antislavery activists fought the law, both in the courts and in their communities. For instance, when Stephen Spencer Hill was seized by his former enslaver, his white neighbors helped free him by distracting his enslaver with food and drink at a hotel.

The Fugitive Slave Law was renewed twice and did not end until 1855, after the peak of the Gold Rush.

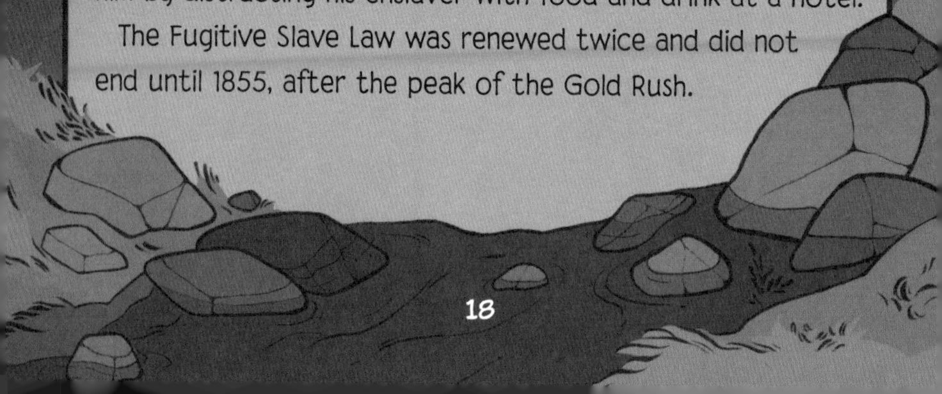

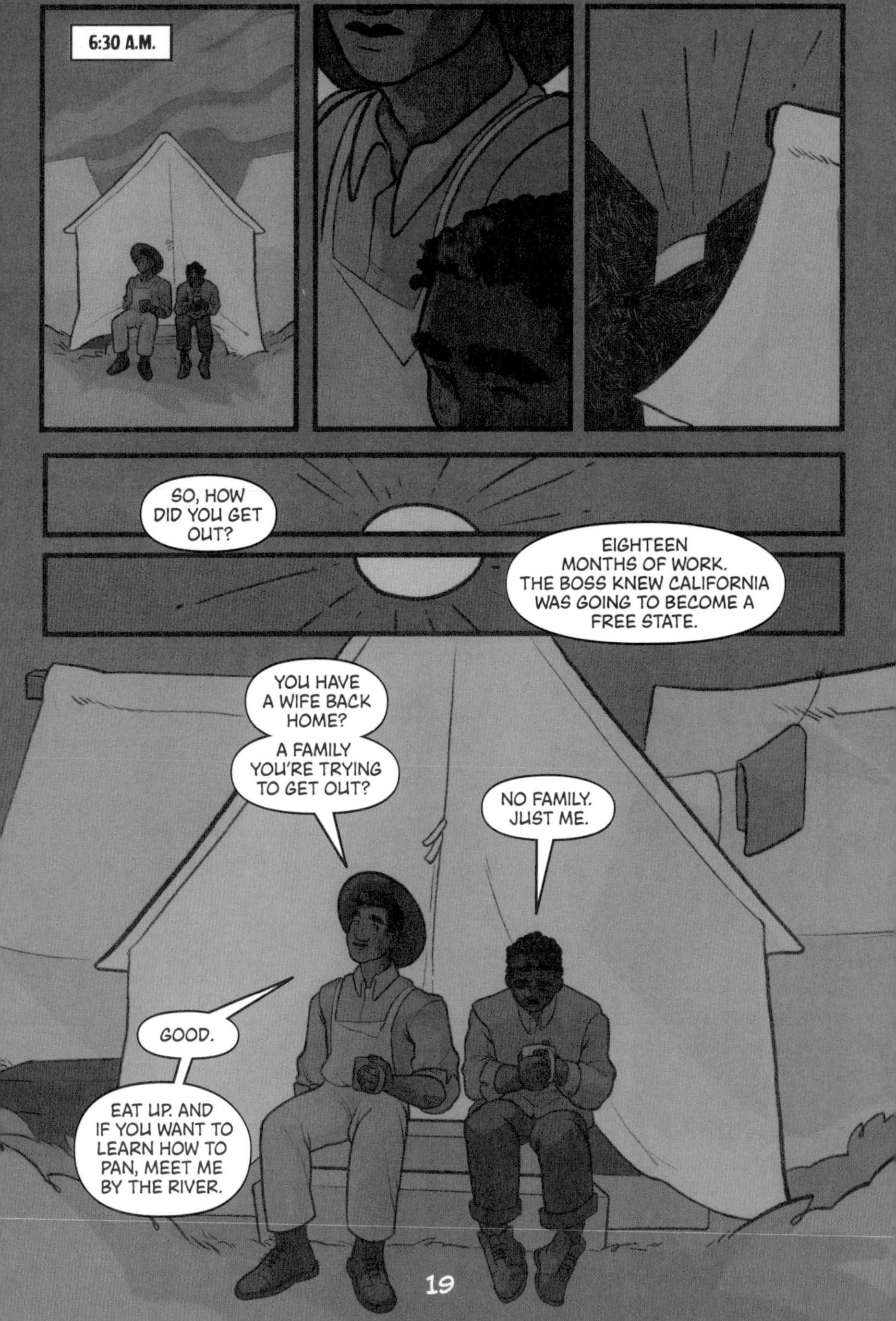
6:30 A.M.
SO, HOW DID YOU GET OUT?
EIGHTEEN MONTHS OF WORK. THE BOSS KNEW CALIFORNIA WAS GOING TO BECOME A FREE STATE.
YOU HAVE A WIFE BACK HOME?
A FAMILY YOU'RE TRYING TO GET OUT?
NO FAMILY. JUST ME.
GOOD.
EAT UP. AND IF YOU WANT TO LEARN HOW TO PAN, MEET ME BY THE RIVER.

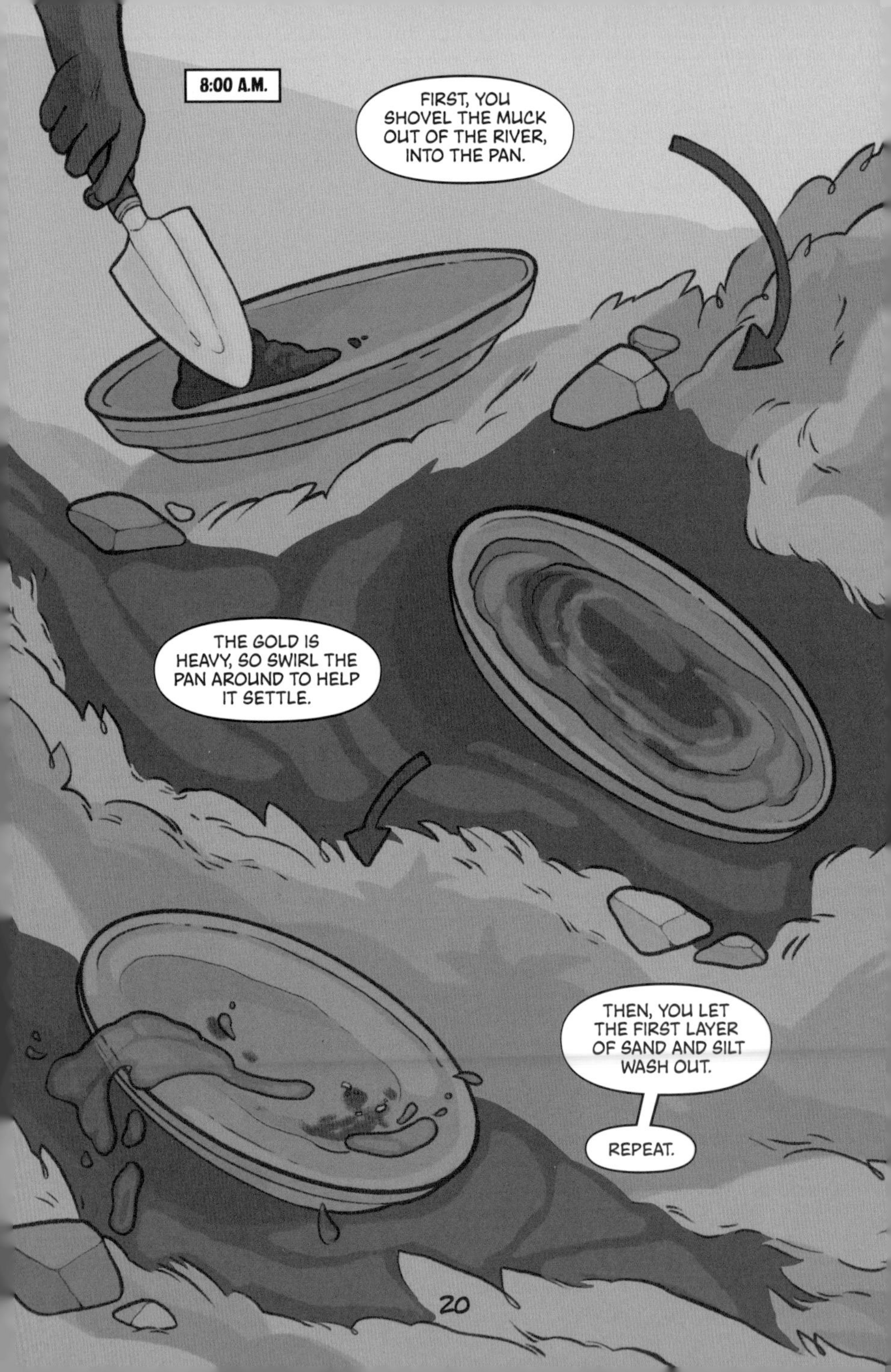

8:00 A.M.
FIRST, YOU SHOVEL THE MUCK OUT OF THE RIVER, INTO THE PAN.
THE GOLD IS HEAVY, SO SWIRL THE PAN AROUND TO HELP IT SETTLE.
THEN, YOU LET THE FIRST LAYER OF SAND AND SILT WASH OUT.
REPEAT.

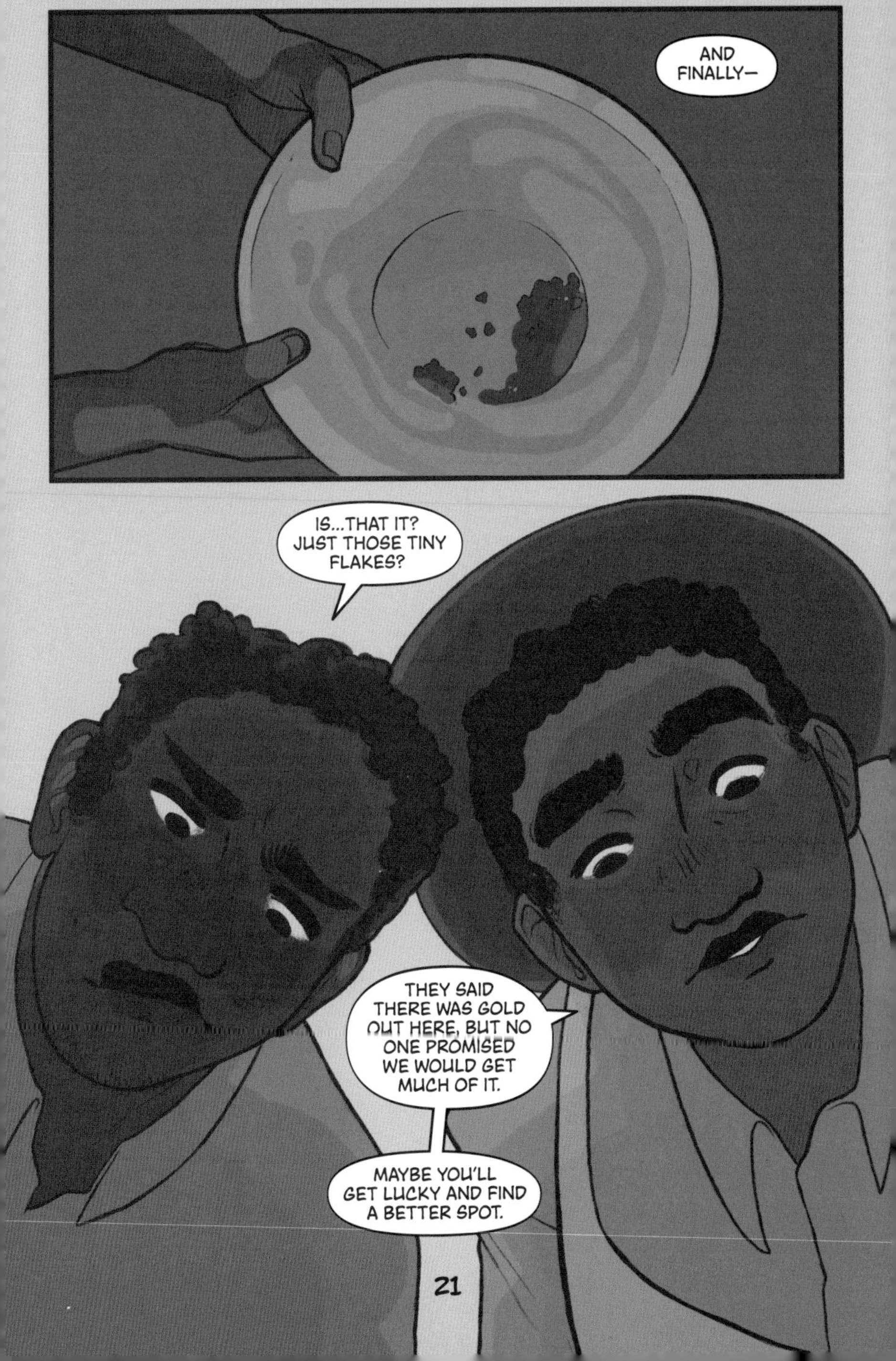
AND FINALLY—
IS...THAT IT? JUST THOSE TINY FLAKES?
THEY SAID THERE WAS GOLD OUT HERE, BUT NO ONE PROMISED WE WOULD GET MUCH OF IT.
MAYBE YOU'LL GET LUCKY AND FIND A BETTER SPOT.

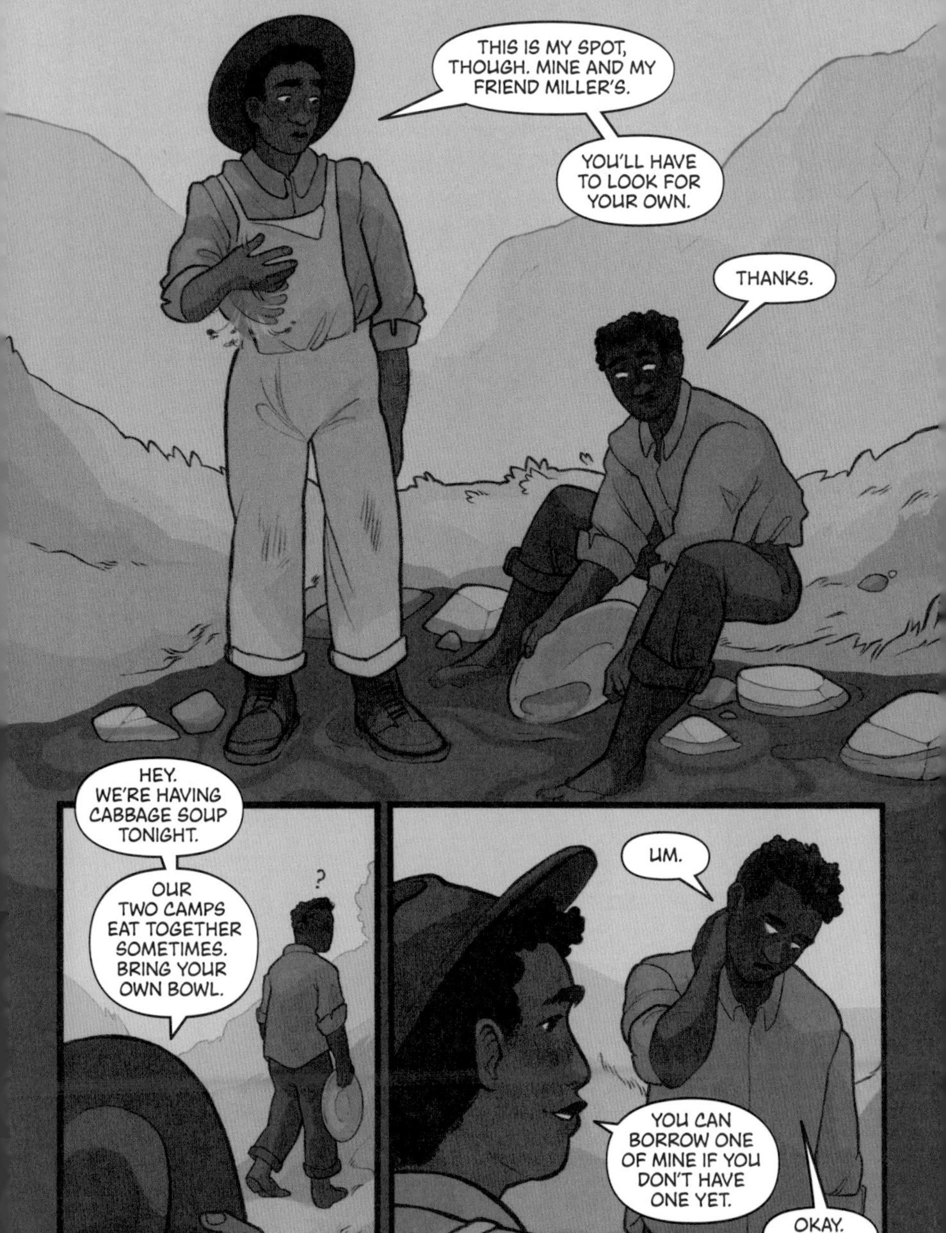
THIS IS MY SPOT, THOUGH. MINE AND MY FRIEND MILLER'S.
YOU'LL HAVE TO LOOK FOR YOUR OWN.
THANKS.
HEY. WE'RE HAVING CABBAGE SOUP TONIGHT.
OUR TWO CAMPS EAT TOGETHER SOMETIMES. BRING YOUR OWN BOWL.
?
UM.
YOU CAN BORROW ONE OF MINE IF YOU DON'T HAVE ONE YET.
OKAY. THANKS.

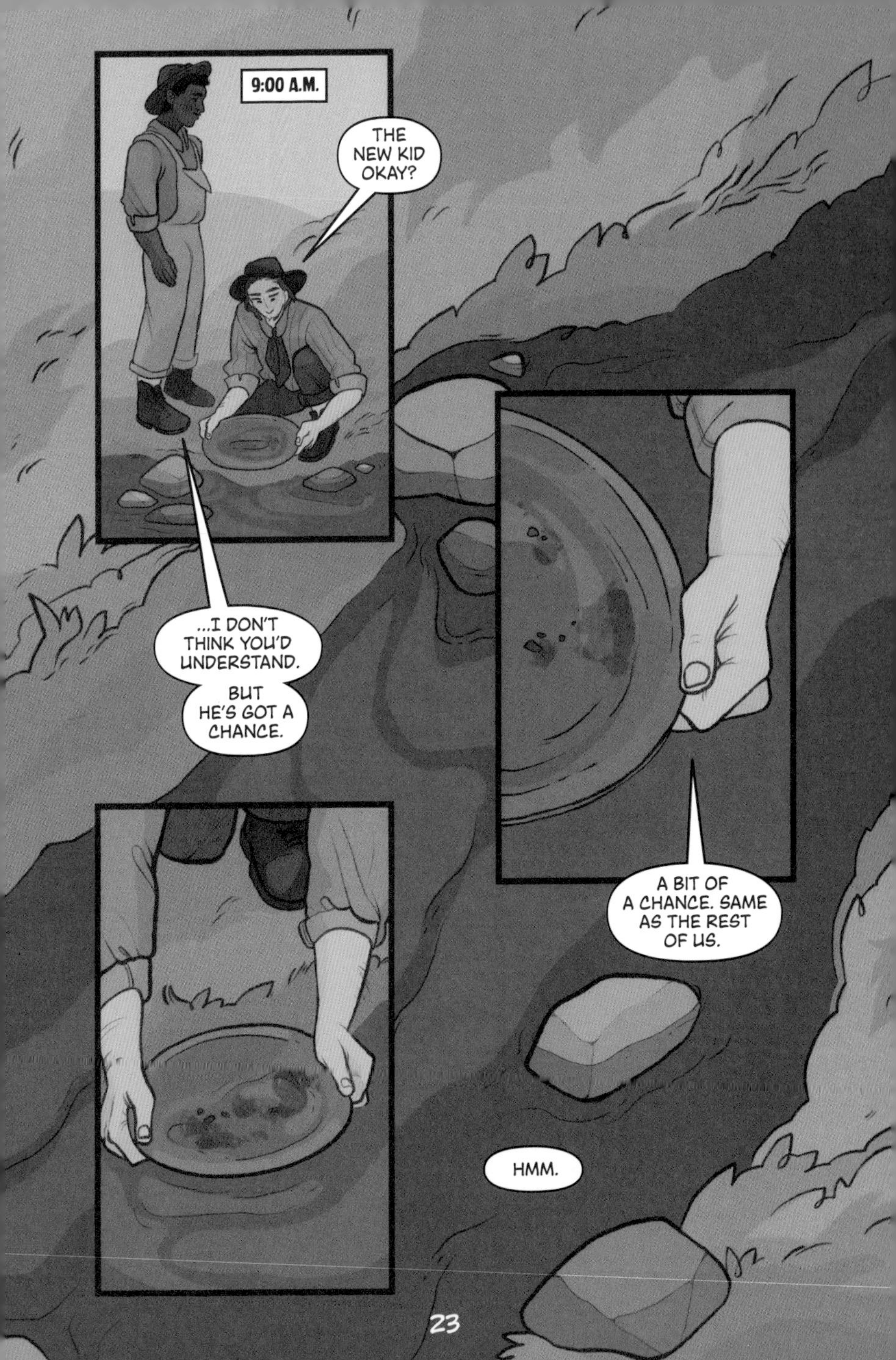
9:00 A.M.
THE NEW KID OKAY?
...I DON'T THINK YOU'D UNDERSTAND.
BUT HE'S GOT A CHANCE.
A BIT OF A CHANCE. SAME AS THE REST OF US.
HMM.

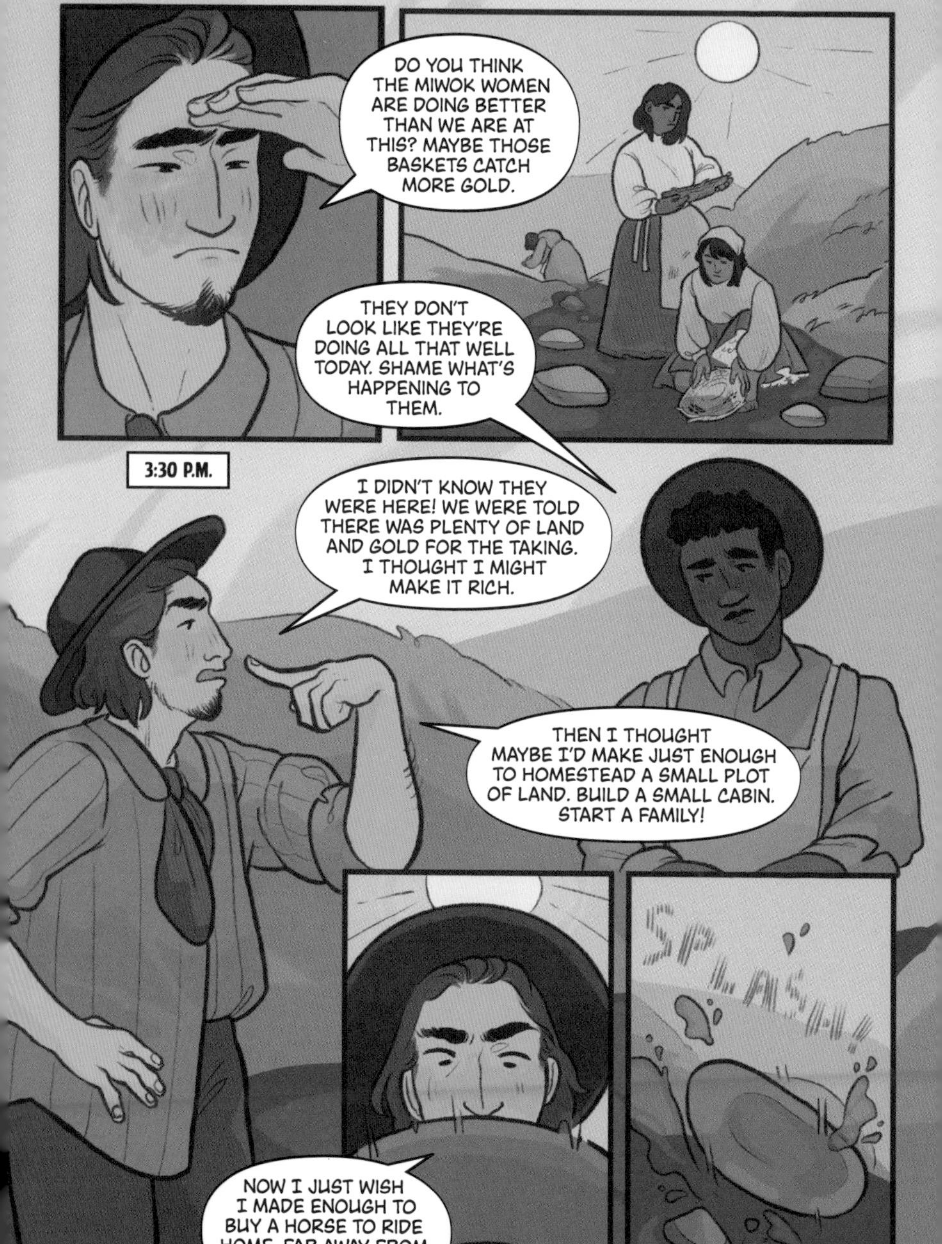
DO YOU THINK THE MIWOK WOMEN ARE DOING BETTER THAN WE ARE AT THIS? MAYBE THOSE BASKETS CATCH MORE GOLD.
THEY DON'T LOOK LIKE THEY'RE DOING ALL THAT WELL TODAY. SHAME WHAT'S HAPPENING TO THEM.
3:30 P.M.
I DIDN'T KNOW THEY WERE HERE! WE WERE TOLD THERE WAS PLENTY OF LAND AND GOLD FOR THE TAKING. I THOUGHT I MIGHT MAKE IT RICH.
THEN I THOUGHT MAYBE I'D MAKE JUST ENOUGH TO HOMESTEAD A SMALL PLOT OF LAND. BUILD A SMALL CABIN. START A FAMILY!
NOW I JUST WISH I MADE ENOUGH TO BUY A HORSE TO RIDE HOME, FAR AWAY FROM THIS BLASTED RIVER!
SPLASH!!

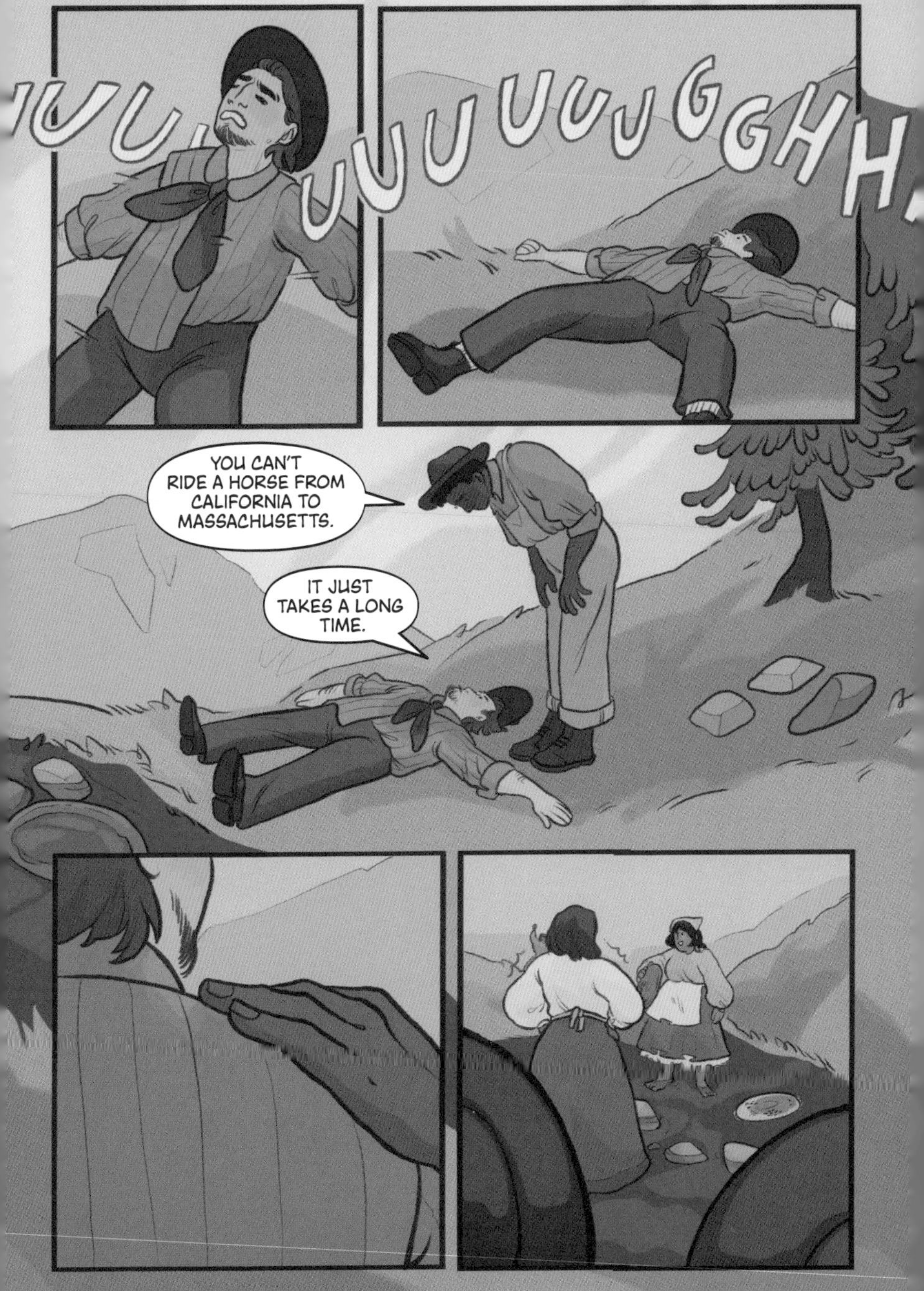
UUUUUUUUUUUGGHH
YOU CAN'T RIDE A HORSE FROM CALIFORNIA TO MASSACHUSETTS.
IT JUST TAKES A LONG TIME.

Indigenous People and the Gold Rush

Indigenous people of North America also mined for gold in the Gold Rush, both independently and as hired workers. They were among the first to travel to the places where gold was discovered, or were often the original inhabitants living in these regions. The Miwok and Yokuts people used woven and coiled grass baskets, which were more effective than metal pans in trapping gold flakes.

White settlers claimed that Indigenous people were uncivilized and savage in order to justify displacing or enslaving them. Unfair trades were struck with them for gold, land, and other resources. Mining destroyed rivers used for fishing, and new settlements ruined Indigenous hunting grounds and sacred lands. In 1850, California passed a law legalizing the enslavement of imprisoned Indigenous people charged with minor offenses and barred them from testifying against white people. The law encouraged white settlers to kidnap, enslave, and even murder Indigenous Californians.

Throughout this period, Indigenous leaders tried to protect their people—some by attempting to forge treaties with the United States government and some by fighting back. Generations of Indigenous people, including the Miwok and Yokuts people, remained in the historical region of the California Gold Rush and continue to live there today.

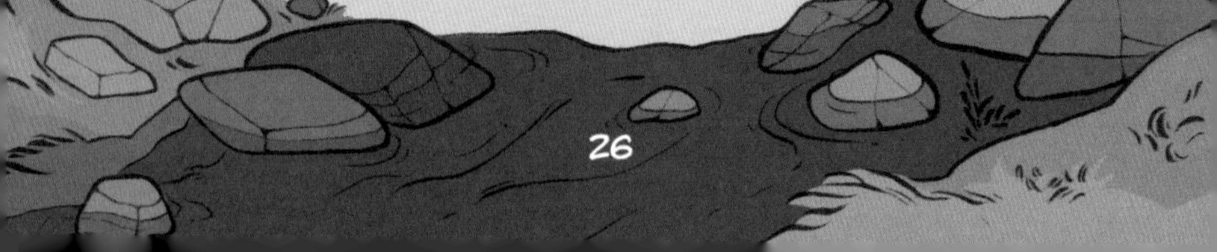

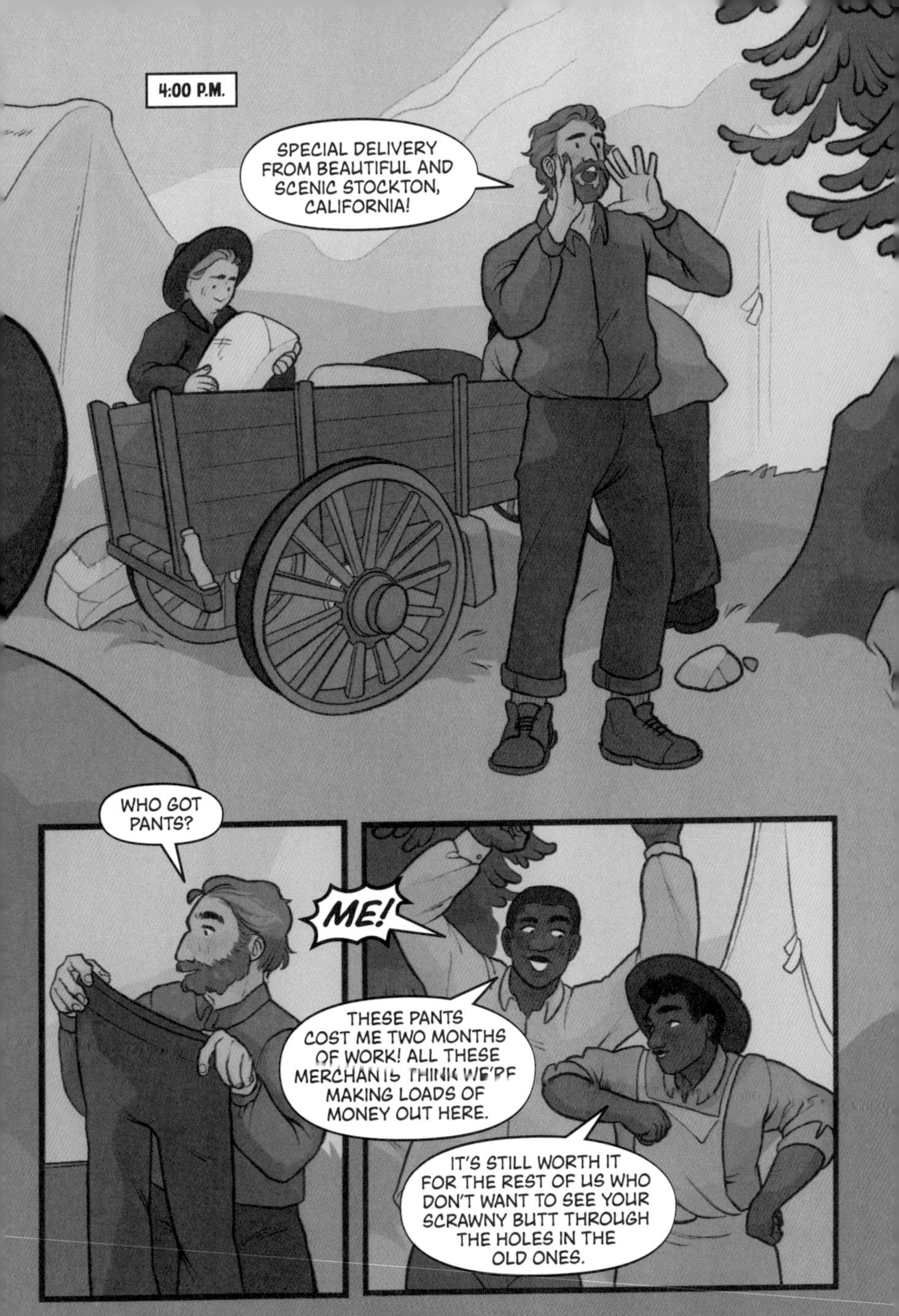
4:00 P.M.
SPECIAL DELIVERY FROM BEAUTIFUL AND SCENIC STOCKTON, CALIFORNIA!
WHO GOT PANTS?
ME!
THESE PANTS COST ME TWO MONTHS OF WORK! ALL THESE MERCHANTS THINK WE'RE MAKING LOADS OF MONEY OUT HERE.
IT'S STILL WORTH IT FOR THE REST OF US WHO DON'T WANT TO SEE YOUR SCRAWNY BUTT THROUGH THE HOLES IN THE OLD ONES.

LEVI STRAUSS GOT HIS START SELLING SUPPLIES TO MINERS DURING THE GOLD RUSH, ALTHOUGH HIS FAMOUS JEANS—WORKPANTS MADE OF HEAVY FABRIC REINFORCED WITH RIVETS—WOULDN'T BE INVENTED BY TAILOR JACOB DAVIS UNTIL 1870.

MOST FOOD HAD TO BE BROUGHT INTO THE GOLDFIELDS, AND AT THE PEAK OF THE GOLD RUSH, PRICES WERE ASTRONOMICAL.

BECAUSE FRESH FRUIT AND VEGETABLES WERE EXPENSIVE AND DIFFICULT TO OBTAIN, MINERS ATE FOOD WITH LITTLE VITAMIN C, AND MANY OF THEM CONTRACTED SCURVY.

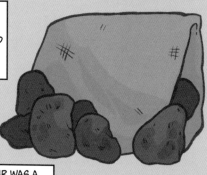

FLOUR WAS A COMMON STAPLE FOOD. IT WAS USED TO MAKE SOURDOUGH BREAD, AND IN LEANER TIMES IT WAS MIXED WITH CORNMEAL AND MILK TO MAKE A SLUDGY MUSH.

MINING EQUIPMENT, SUCH AS PANS AND SHOVELS, WAS SOLD AT VERY HIGH PRICES.

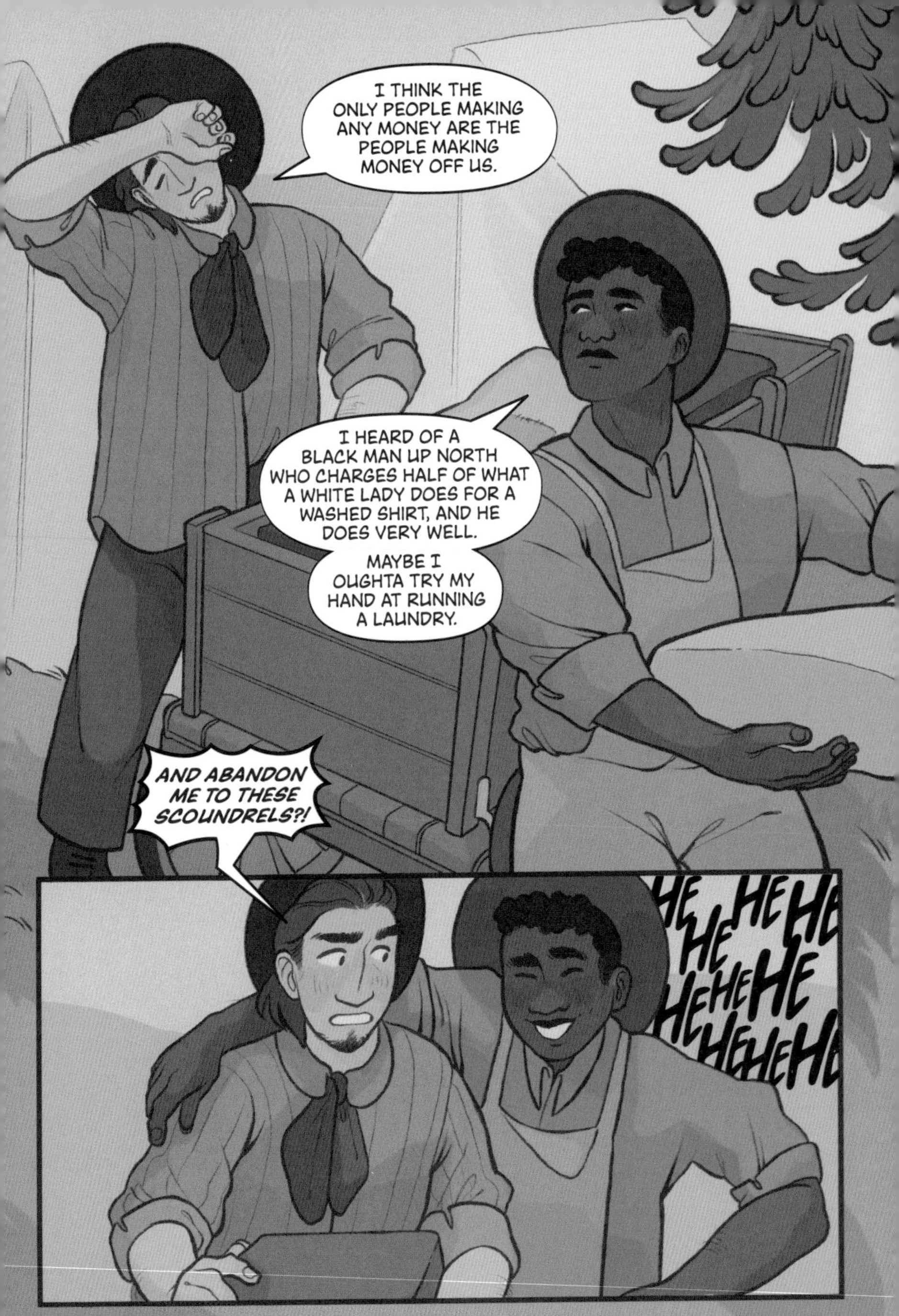
I THINK THE ONLY PEOPLE MAKING ANY MONEY ARE THE PEOPLE MAKING MONEY OFF US.
I HEARD OF A BLACK MAN UP NORTH WHO CHARGES HALF OF WHAT A WHITE LADY DOES FOR A WASHED SHIRT, AND HE DOES VERY WELL.
MAYBE I OUGHTA TRY MY HAND AT RUNNING A LAUNDRY.
AND ABANDON ME TO THESE SCOUNDRELS?!
HEHEHEHEHEHEHEHEHEHEHEHE

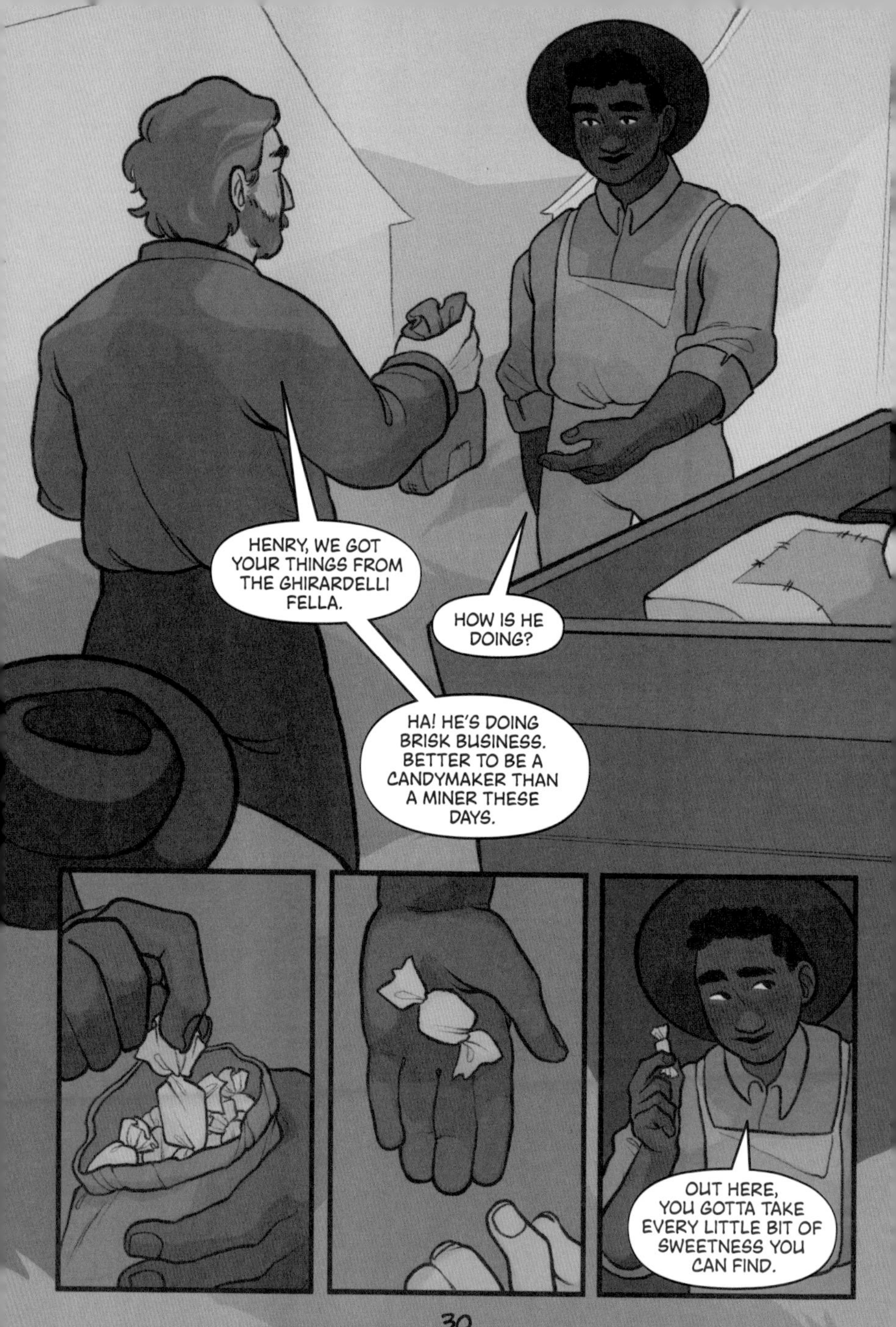
HENRY, WE GOT YOUR THINGS FROM THE GHIRARDELLI FELLA.
HOW IS HE DOING?
HA! HE'S DOING BRISK BUSINESS. BETTER TO BE A CANDYMAKER THAN A MINER THESE DAYS.
OUT HERE, YOU GOTTA TAKE EVERY LITTLE BIT OF SWEETNESS YOU CAN FIND.

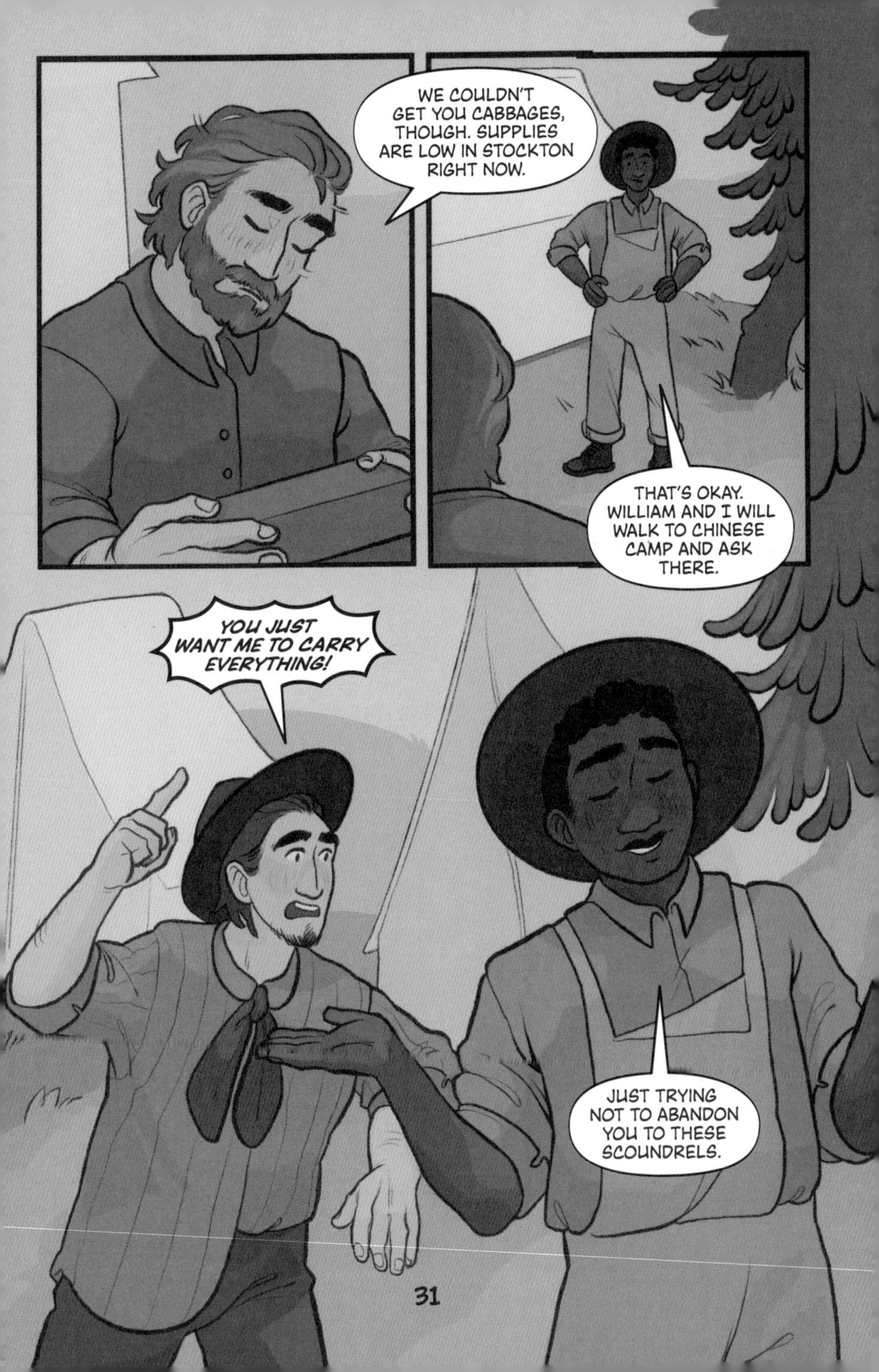
WE COULDN'T GET YOU CABBAGES, THOUGH. SUPPLIES ARE LOW IN STOCKTON RIGHT NOW.
THAT'S OKAY. WILLIAM AND I WILL WALK TO CHINESE CAMP AND ASK THERE.
YOU JUST WANT ME TO CARRY EVERYTHING!
JUST TRYING NOT TO ABANDON YOU TO THESE SCOUNDRELS.

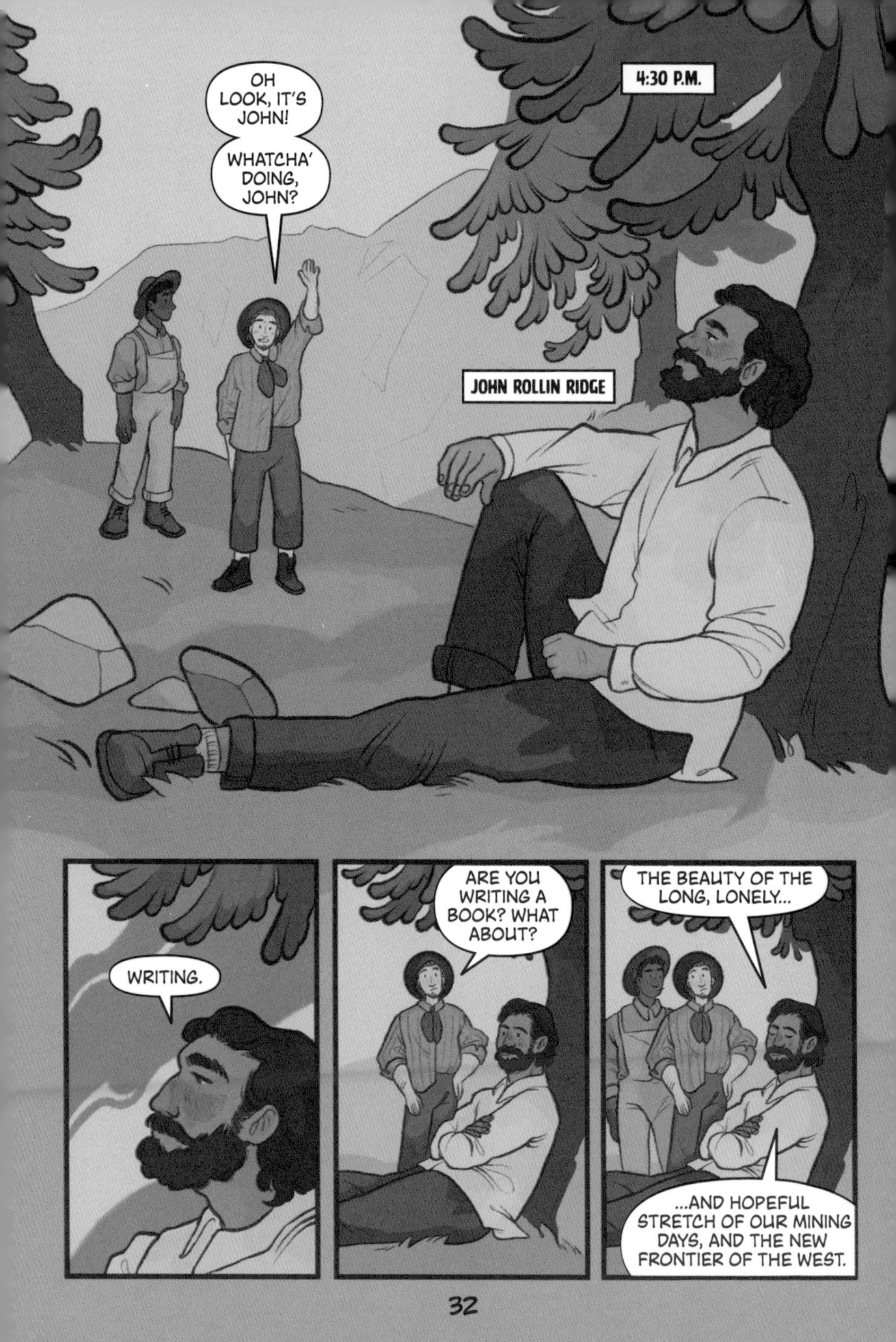
OH LOOK, IT'S JOHN!
WHATCHA' DOING, JOHN?
4:30 P.M.
JOHN ROLLIN RIDGE
WRITING.
ARE YOU WRITING A BOOK? WHAT ABOUT?
THE BEAUTY OF THE LONG, LONELY...
...AND HOPEFUL STRETCH OF OUR MINING DAYS, AND THE NEW FRONTIER OF THE WEST.

John Rollin Ridge

John Rollin Ridge was born in 1827 in New Echota, then the capital of the Cherokee Nation, of which he was a member. John traveled west not only to be part of the Gold Rush, but also to avoid trouble with the law out east.

When he arrived in California in 1850, he quickly realized he hated mining, but always had a knack for writing.

In 1854, John published his novel, *The Life and Adventures of Joaquín Murieta: The Celebrated California Bandit*, which he wrote under the name Yellow Bird, a translation of his Cherokee name, Cheesquatalawny (say: chee-squa-ta-law-ny). The book is about a young Mexican man who tries his luck mining during the California Gold Rush, but after facing racism and violence from white Americans, becomes an infamous bandit. It is one of the first novels published in California, and John is considered to be the first Native American novelist.

In the novel, John criticizes the racism toward Mexicans in California, but the anti-racist views in his writing were not reflected in his life. He had enslaved people in Arkansas, and during the Civil War, he voiced his support for the Confederacy, which had promised Native Americans their own state if the South won the war. After the Union's victory, John was part of a Cherokee delegation that negotiated a peace treaty with the United States.

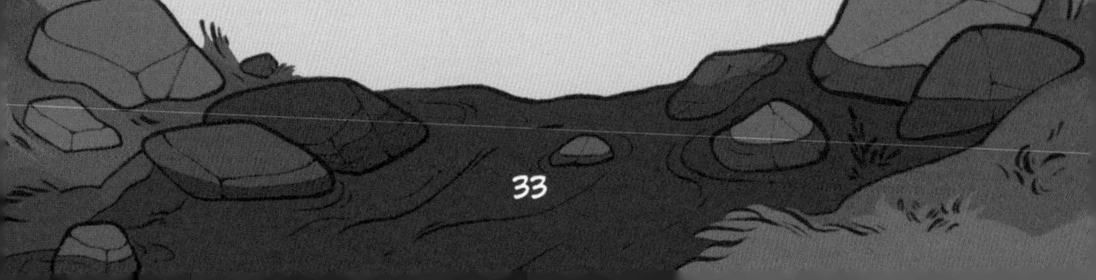

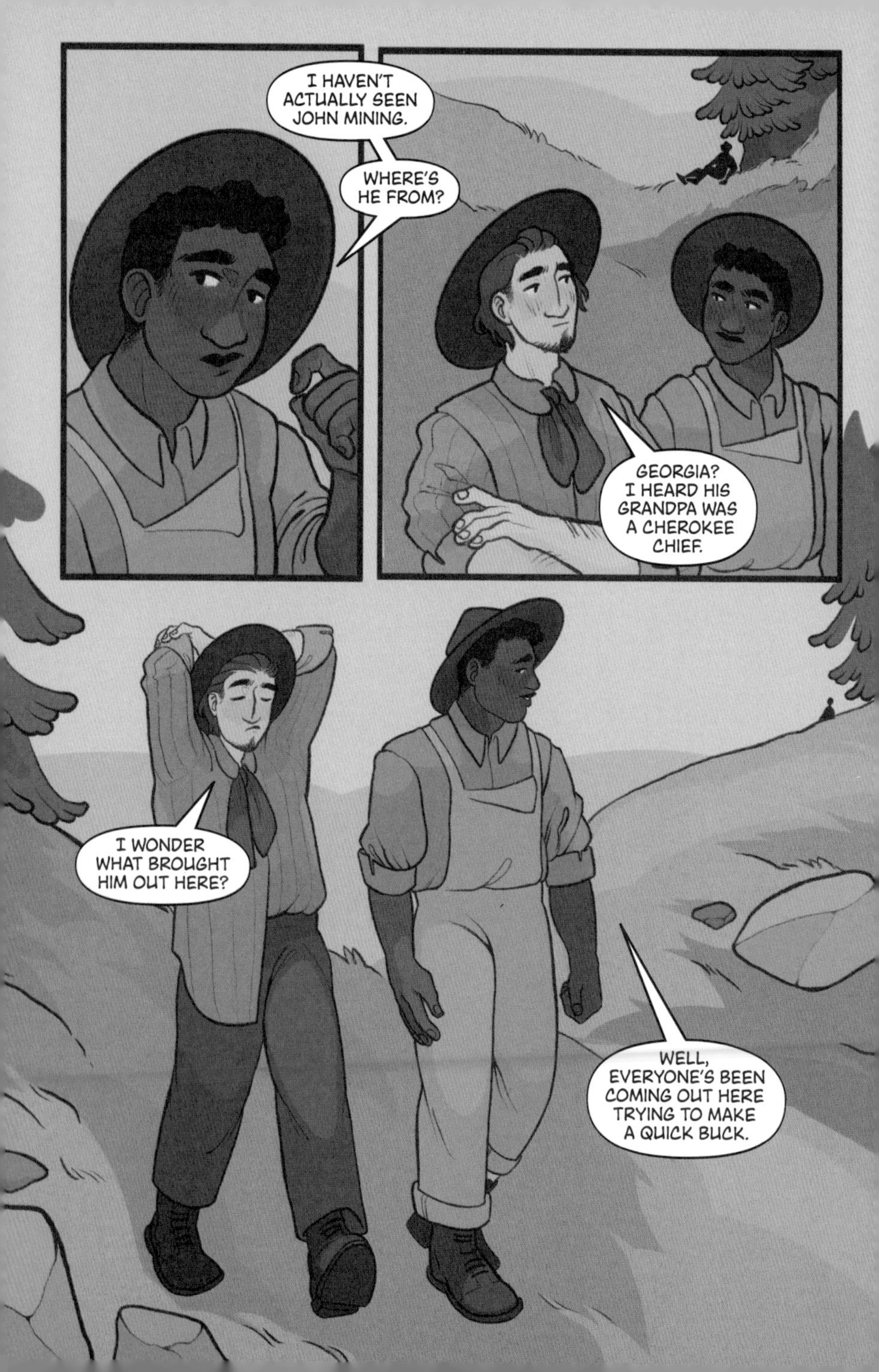
I HAVEN'T ACTUALLY SEEN JOHN MINING.
WHERE'S HE FROM?
GEORGIA? I HEARD HIS GRANDPA WAS A CHEROKEE CHIEF.
I WONDER WHAT BROUGHT HIM OUT HERE?
WELL, EVERYONE'S BEEN COMING OUT HERE TRYING TO MAKE A QUICK BUCK.

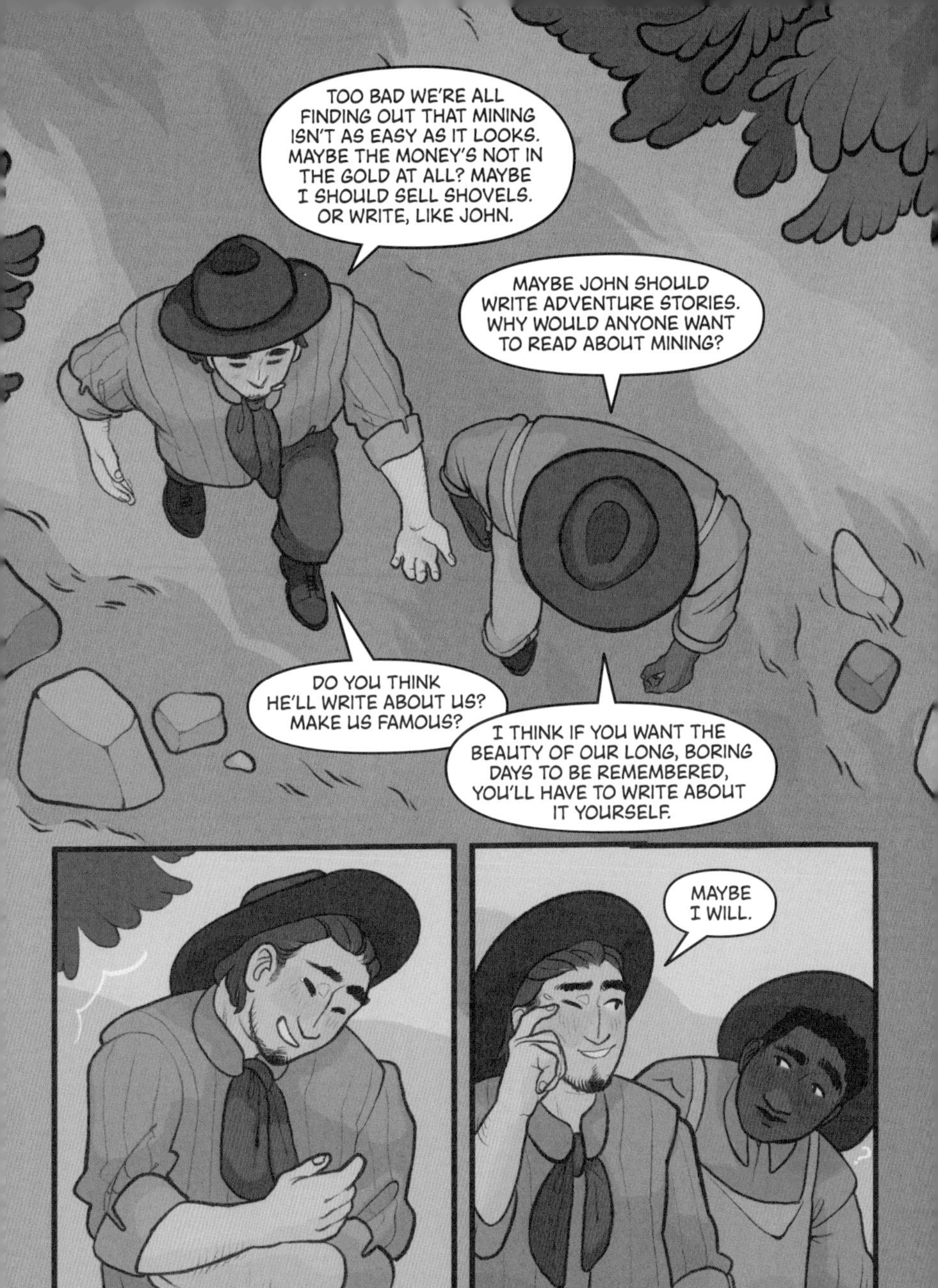
TOO BAD WE'RE ALL FINDING OUT THAT MINING ISN'T AS EASY AS IT LOOKS. MAYBE THE MONEY'S NOT IN THE GOLD AT ALL? MAYBE I SHOULD SELL SHOVELS. OR WRITE, LIKE JOHN.
MAYBE JOHN SHOULD WRITE ADVENTURE STORIES. WHY WOULD ANYONE WANT TO READ ABOUT MINING?
DO YOU THINK HE'LL WRITE ABOUT US? MAKE US FAMOUS?
I THINK IF YOU WANT THE BEAUTY OF OUR LONG, BORING DAYS TO BE REMEMBERED, YOU'LL HAVE TO WRITE ABOUT IT YOURSELF.
MAYBE I WILL.

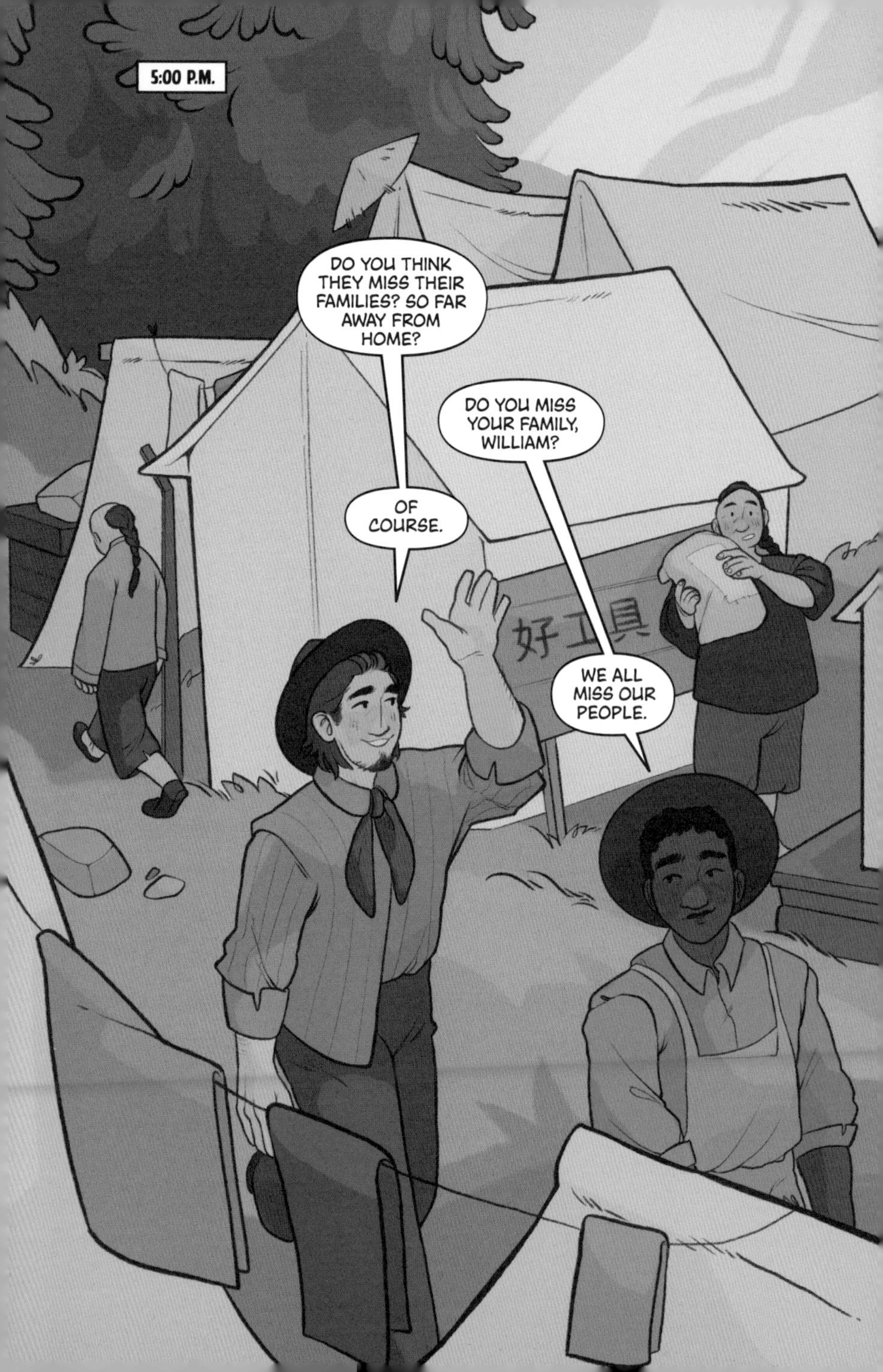
5:00 P.M.
DO YOU THINK THEY MISS THEIR FAMILIES? SO FAR AWAY FROM HOME?
OF COURSE.
DO YOU MISS YOUR FAMILY, WILLIAM?
WE ALL MISS OUR PEOPLE.
好工員

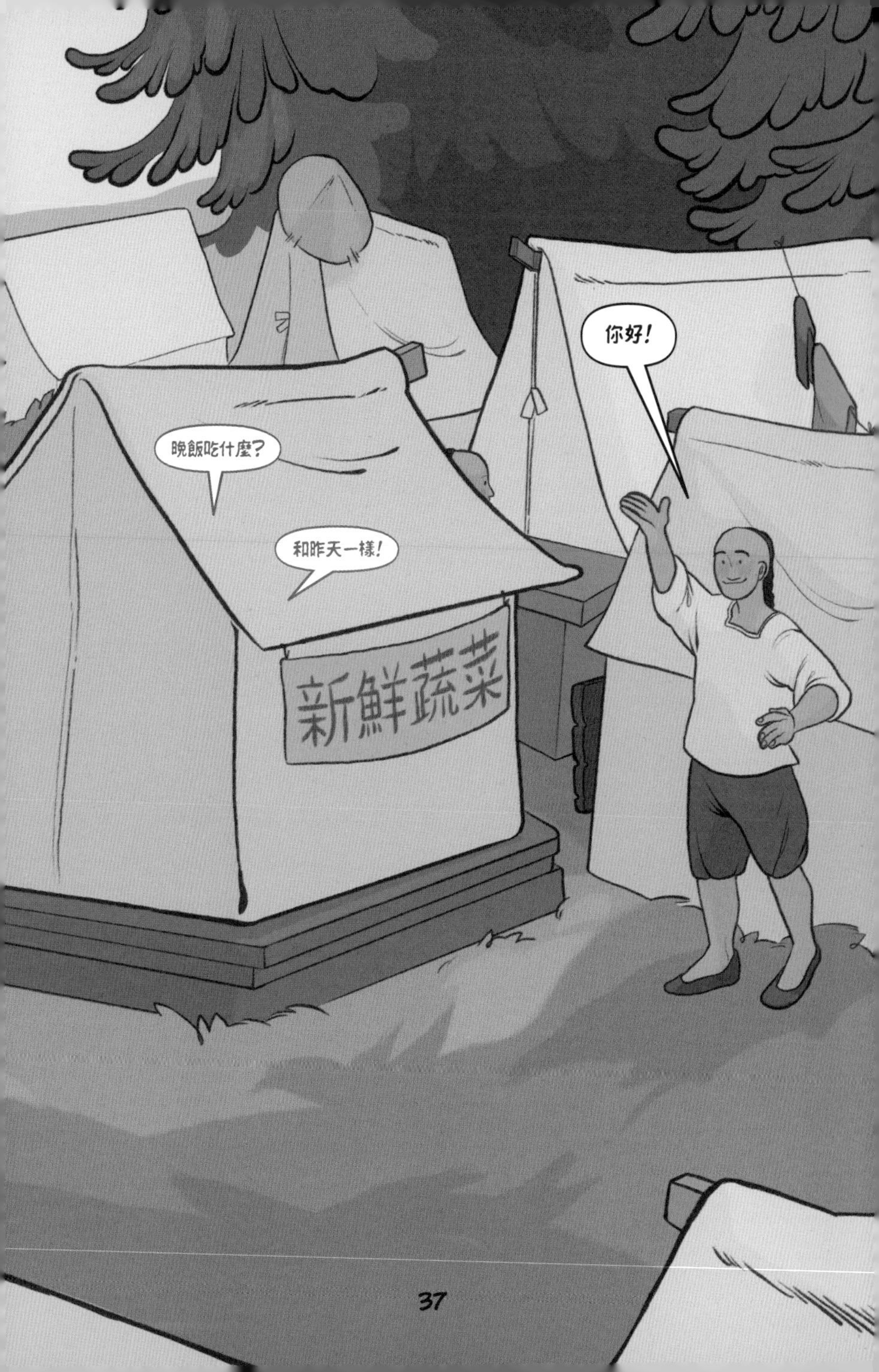

你好！
晚飯吃什麼？
和昨天一樣！
新鮮蔬菜

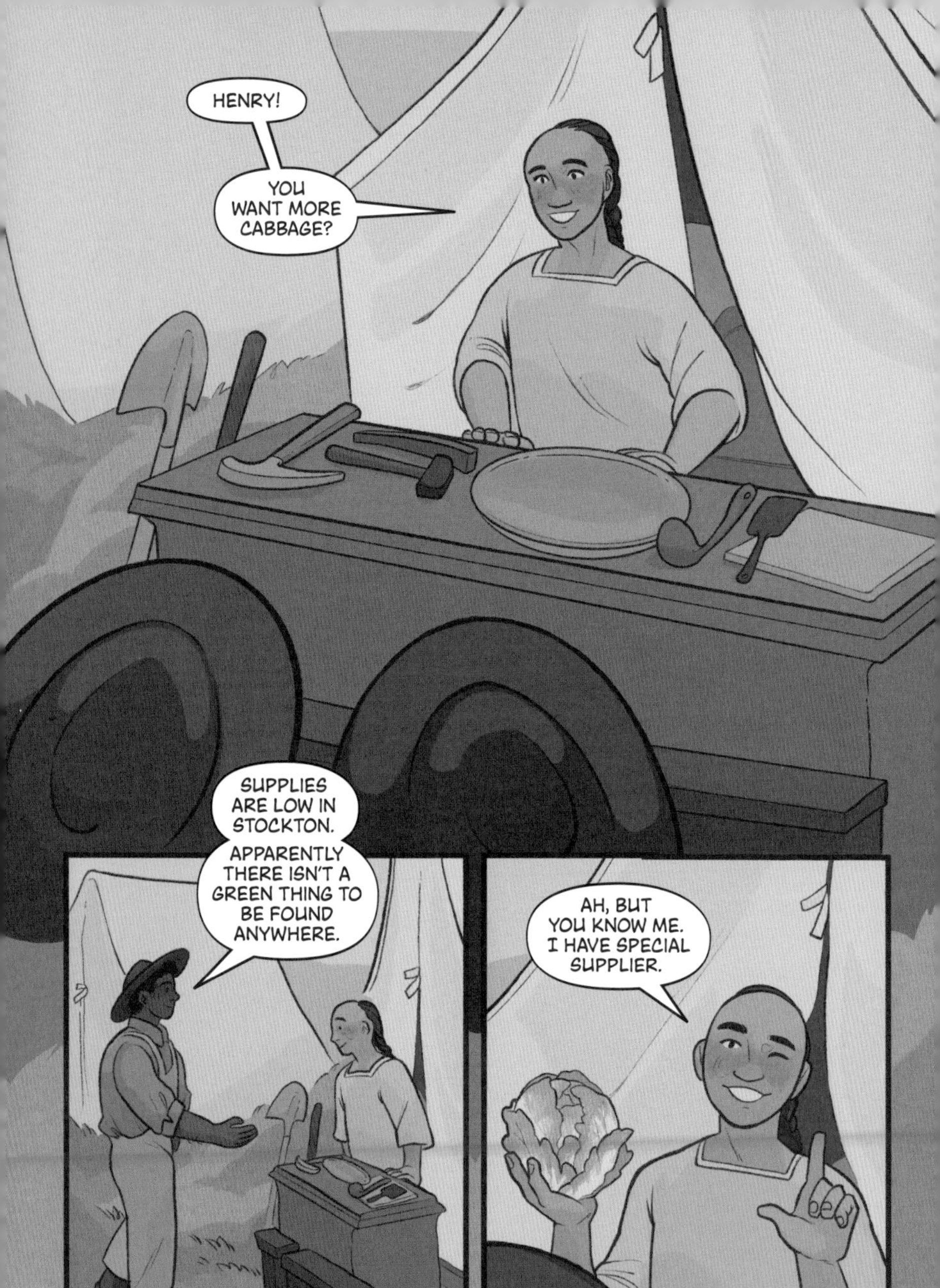
HENRY!
YOU WANT MORE CABBAGE?
SUPPLIES ARE LOW IN STOCKTON.
APPARENTLY THERE ISN'T A GREEN THING TO BE FOUND ANYWHERE.
AH, BUT YOU KNOW ME. I HAVE SPECIAL SUPPLIER.

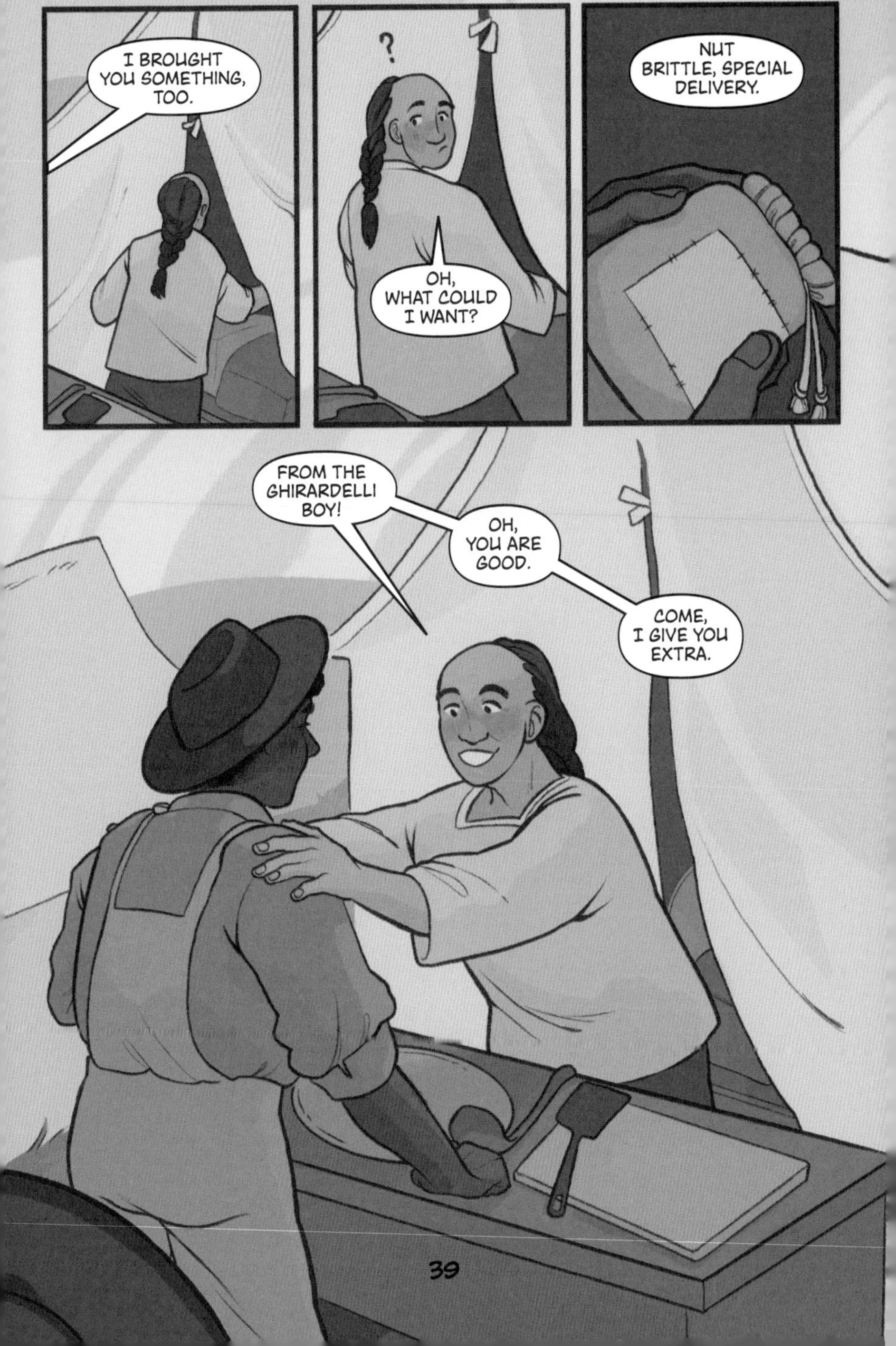
I BROUGHT YOU SOMETHING, TOO.
?
OH, WHAT COULD I WANT?
NUT BRITTLE, SPECIAL DELIVERY.
FROM THE GHIRARDELLI BOY!
OH, YOU ARE GOOD.
COME, I GIVE YOU EXTRA.

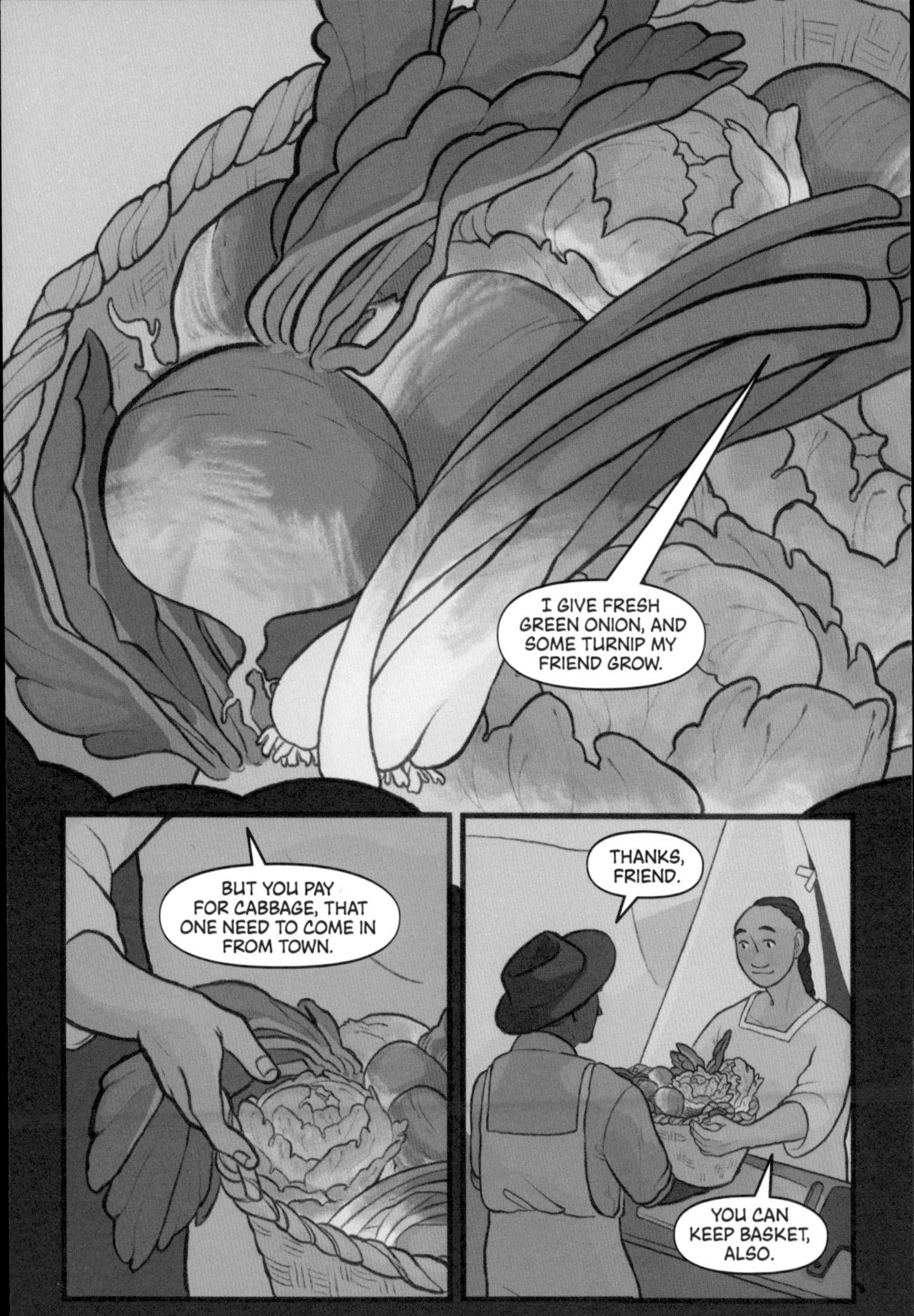
I GIVE FRESH GREEN ONION, AND SOME TURNIP MY FRIEND GROW.
BUT YOU PAY FOR CABBAGE, THAT ONE NEED TO COME IN FROM TOWN.
THANKS, FRIEND.
YOU CAN KEEP BASKET, ALSO.

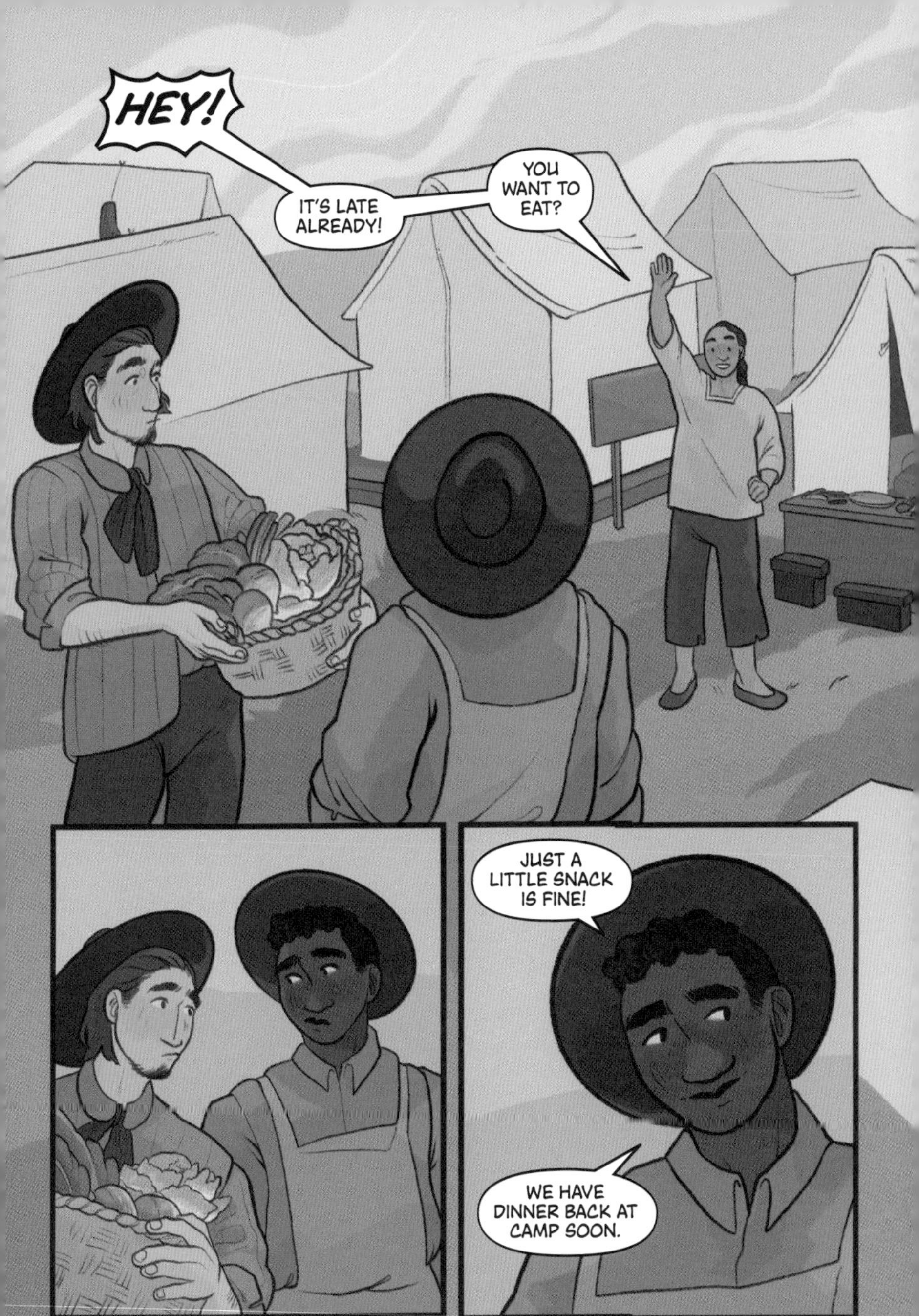
HEY!
IT'S LATE ALREADY!
YOU WANT TO EAT?
JUST A LITTLE SNACK IS FINE!
WE HAVE DINNER BACK AT CAMP SOON.

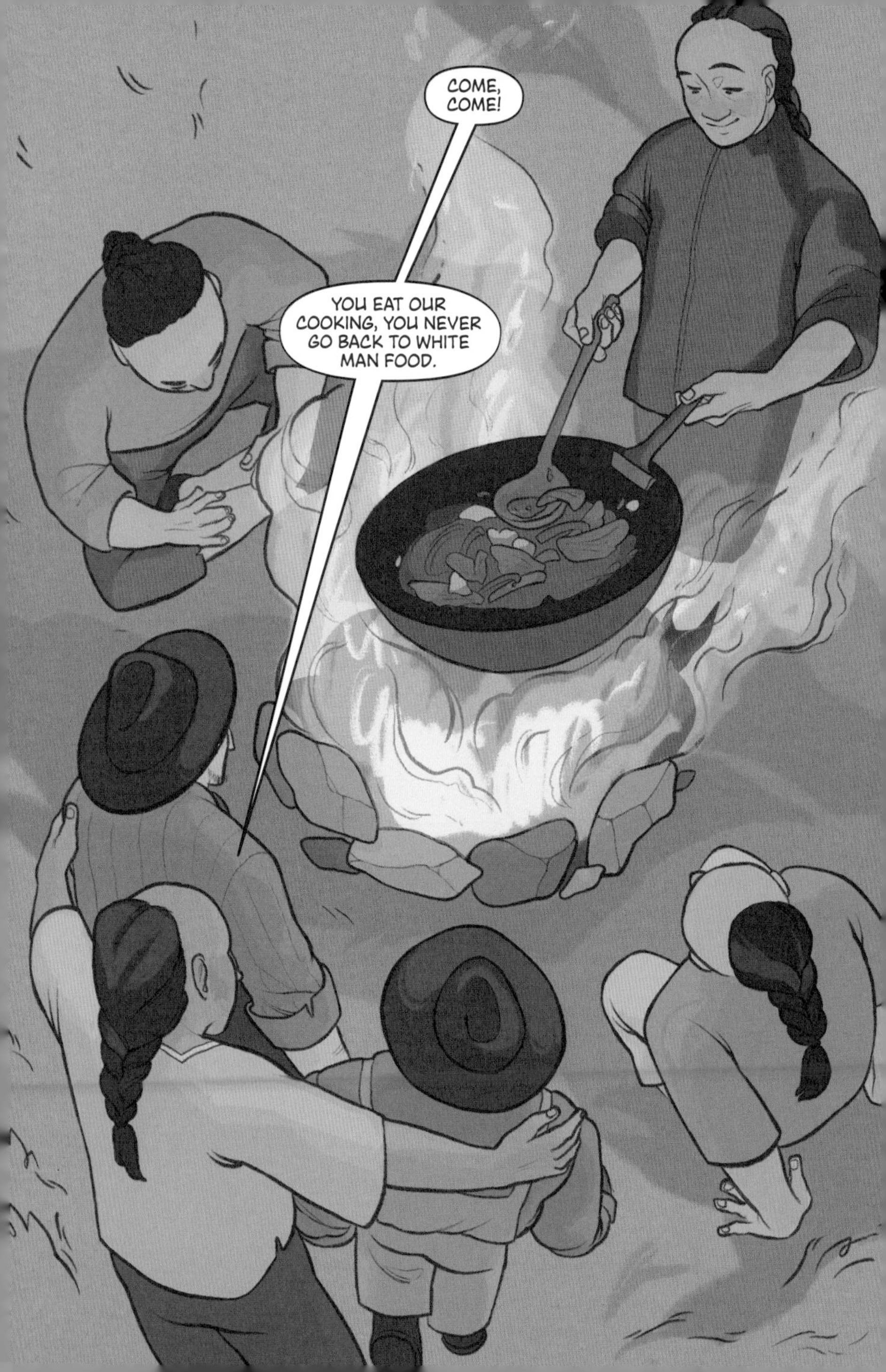
COME, COME!
YOU EAT OUR COOKING, YOU NEVER GO BACK TO WHITE MAN FOOD.

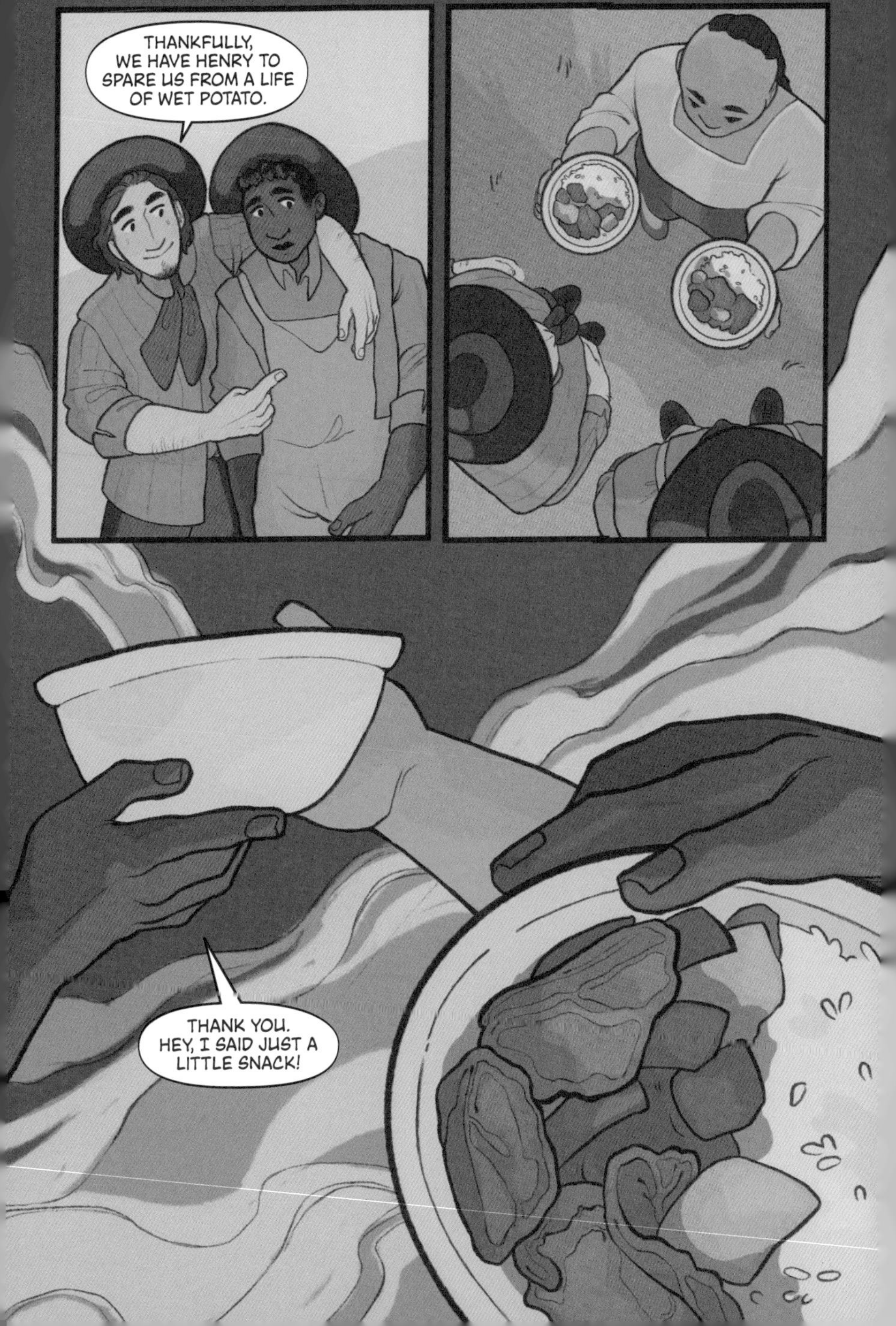
THANKFULLY, WE HAVE HENRY TO SPARE US FROM A LIFE OF WET POTATO.
THANK YOU. HEY, I SAID JUST A LITTLE SNACK!

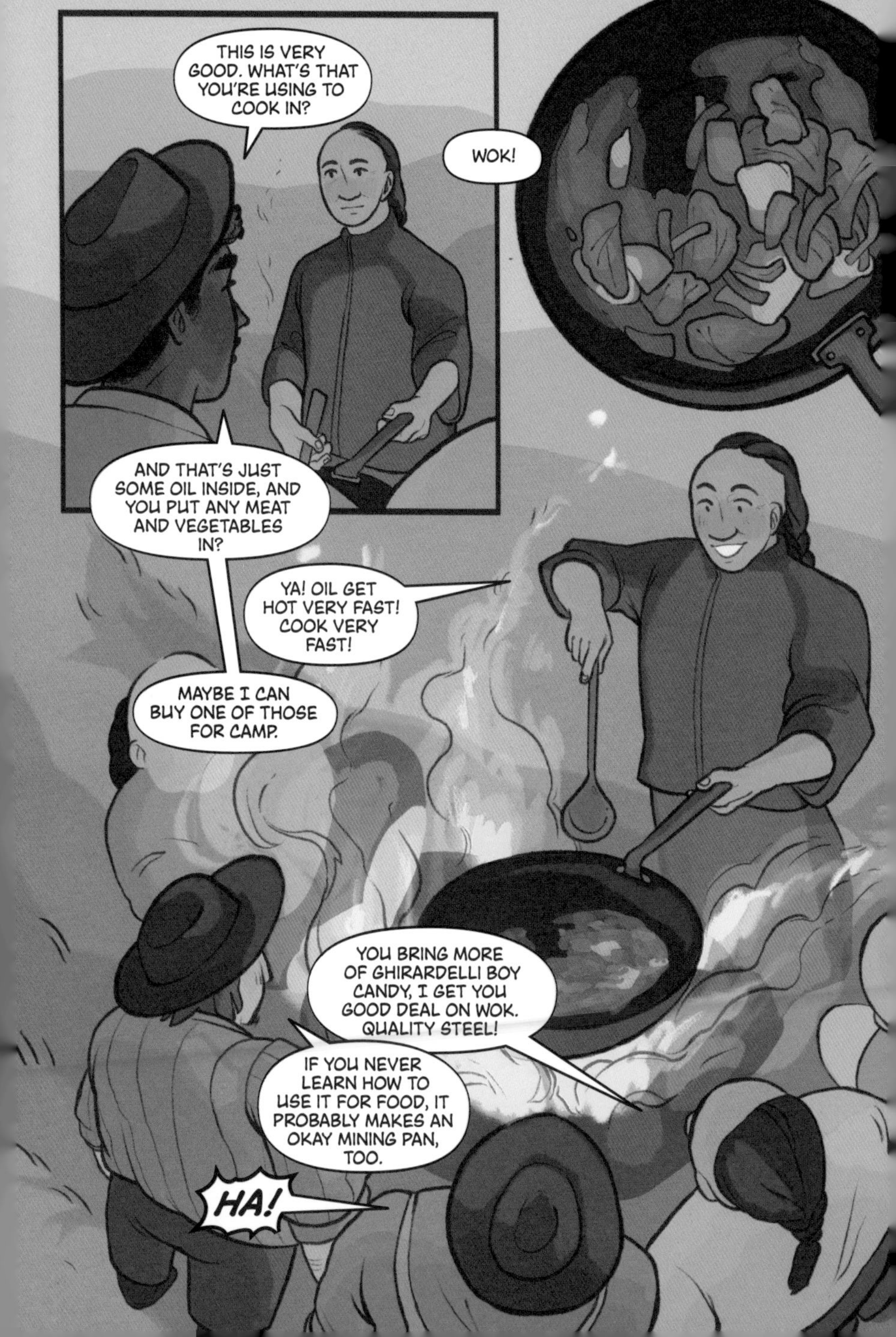
THIS IS VERY GOOD. WHAT'S THAT YOU'RE USING TO COOK IN?
WOK!
AND THAT'S JUST SOME OIL INSIDE, AND YOU PUT ANY MEAT AND VEGETABLES IN?
YA! OIL GET HOT VERY FAST! COOK VERY FAST!
MAYBE I CAN BUY ONE OF THOSE FOR CAMP.
YOU BRING MORE OF GHIRARDELLI BOY CANDY, I GET YOU GOOD DEAL ON WOK. QUALITY STEEL!
IF YOU NEVER LEARN HOW TO USE IT FOR FOOD, IT PROBABLY MAKES AN OKAY MINING PAN, TOO.
HA!

Chinese Immigration and the Gold Rush

At the height of Gold Rush immigration in 1852, twenty thousand Chinese people immigrated to California, and by the end of the 1850s, Chinese immigrants made up one-fifth of the population in the Southern Mines. Some Chinese men found that cooking and washing laundry, tasks primarily done by women, were reliable ways to make money and opened laundries and restaurants instead of mining.

With the rise in immigration, particularly Latin American and Chinese immigration, came a rise in anti-immigrant views. Soon after the Gold Rush began, the Foreign Miners' Tax Act of 1850 was passed, which charged foreign, primarily Spanish-speaking miners a monthly tax of twenty dollars—the equivalent of several hundred dollars today. Following protests from Irish, English, Canadian, and German miners, any "free white person" became exempt. In 1852, a new version of the tax targeted Chinese immigrants, forcing many of them to leave the goldfields for more populated areas, establishing Chinatowns in cities like San Francisco.

After the peak of the Gold Rush, many Chinese men would go on to work for the Central Pacific Railroad, which actively recruited laborers from China, with up to twenty thousand Chinese migrants working on the first transcontinental railroad from 1863 to 1869.

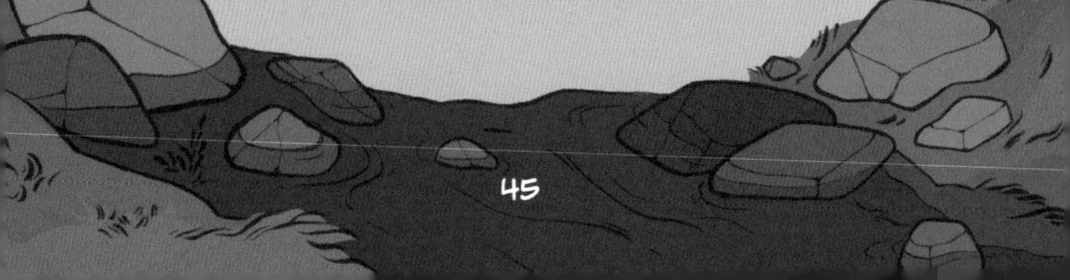

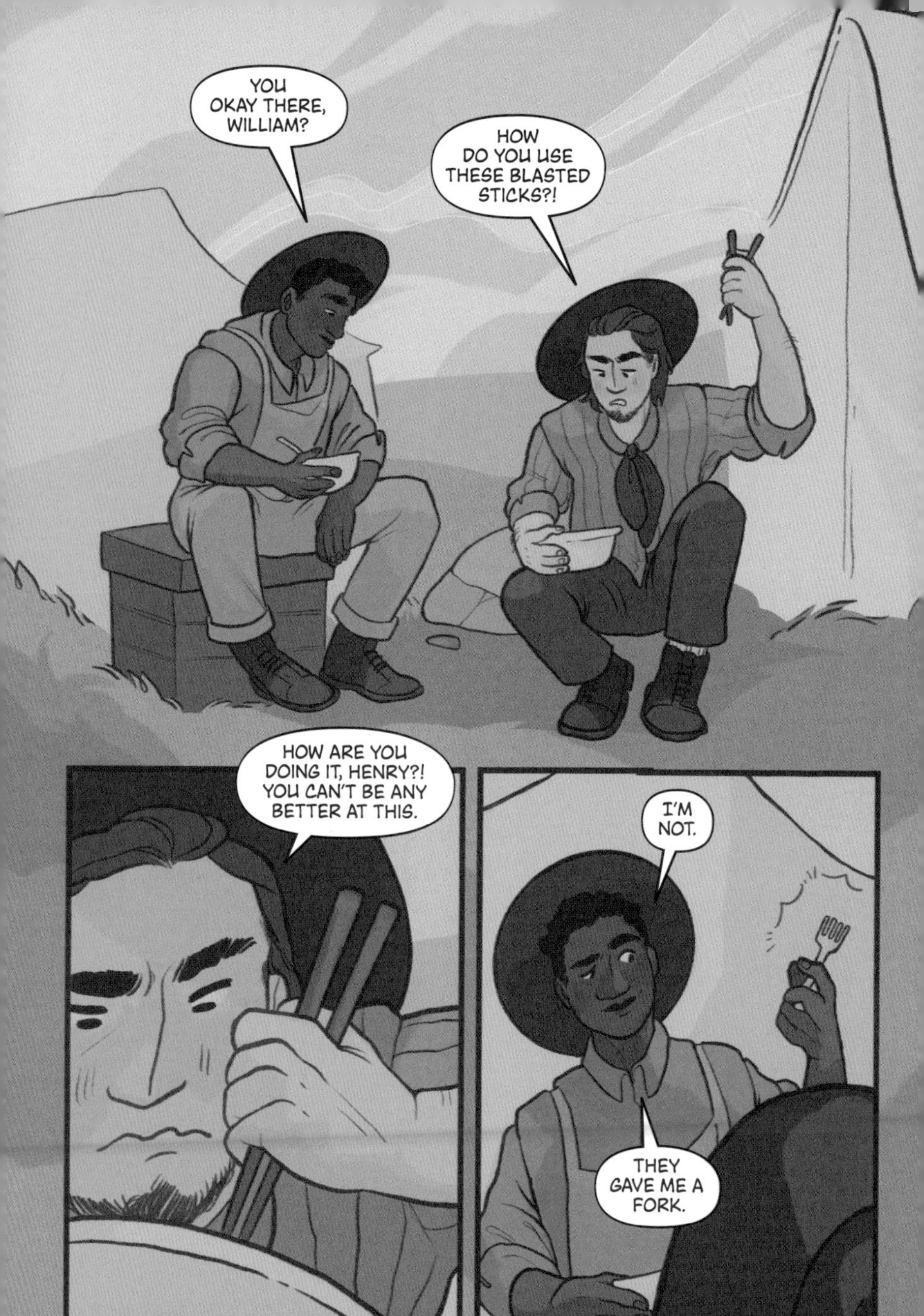
YOU OKAY THERE, WILLIAM?
HOW DO YOU USE THESE BLASTED STICKS?!
HOW ARE YOU DOING IT, HENRY?! YOU CAN'T BE ANY BETTER AT THIS.
I'M NOT.
THEY GAVE ME A FORK.

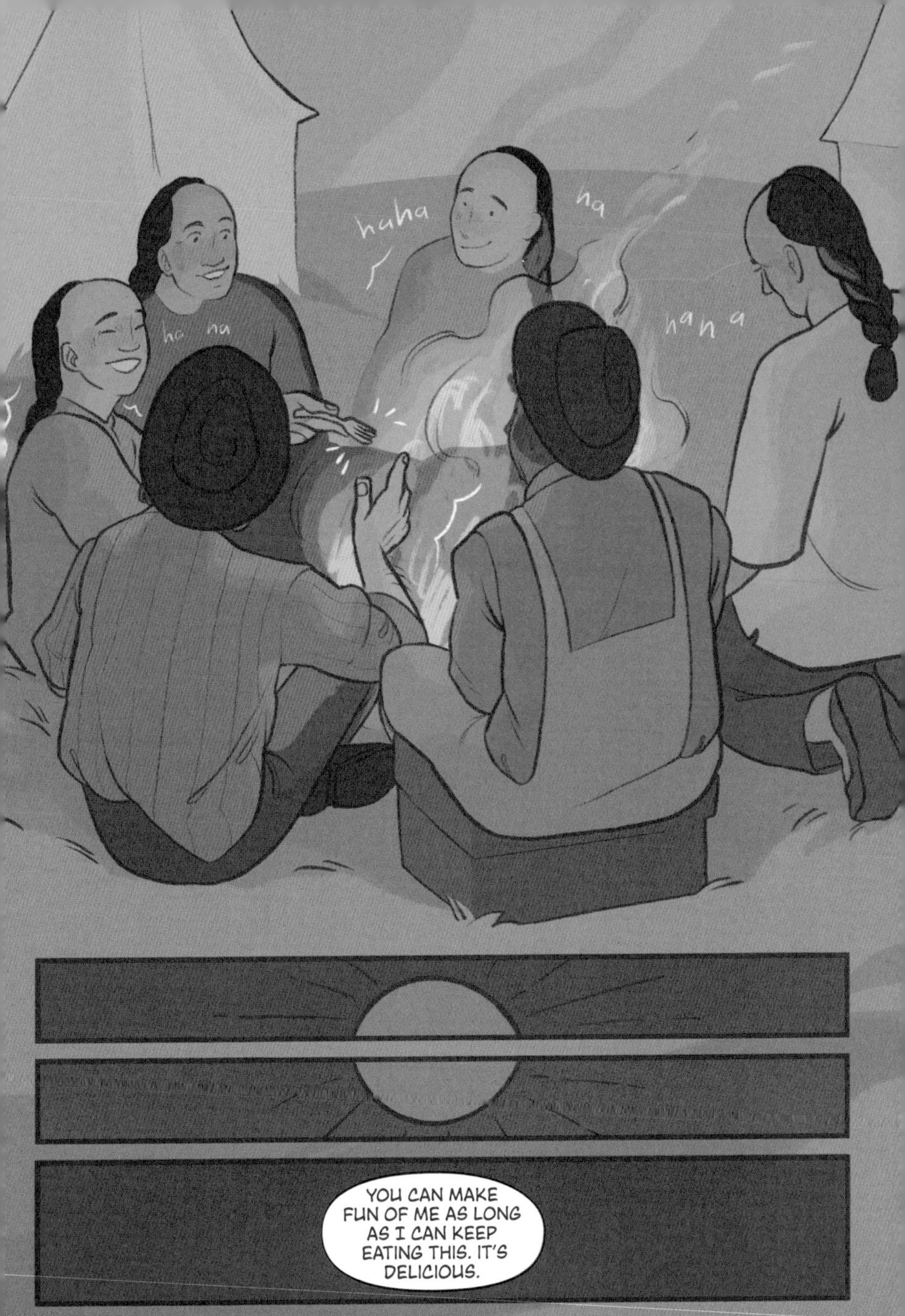
haha
ha
ha ha
han a
YOU CAN MAKE FUN OF ME AS LONG AS I CAN KEEP EATING THIS. IT'S DELICIOUS.

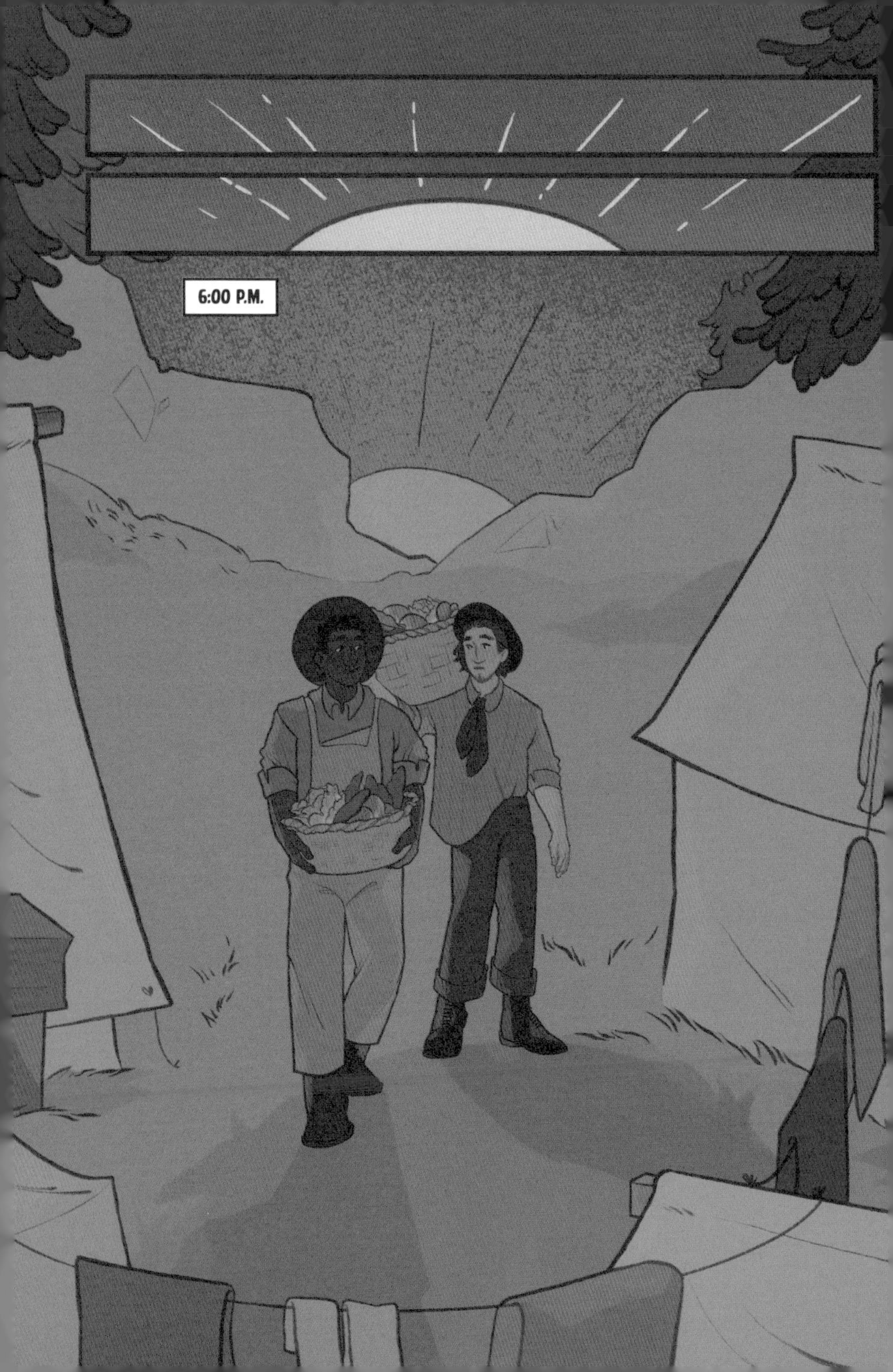
6:00 P.M.

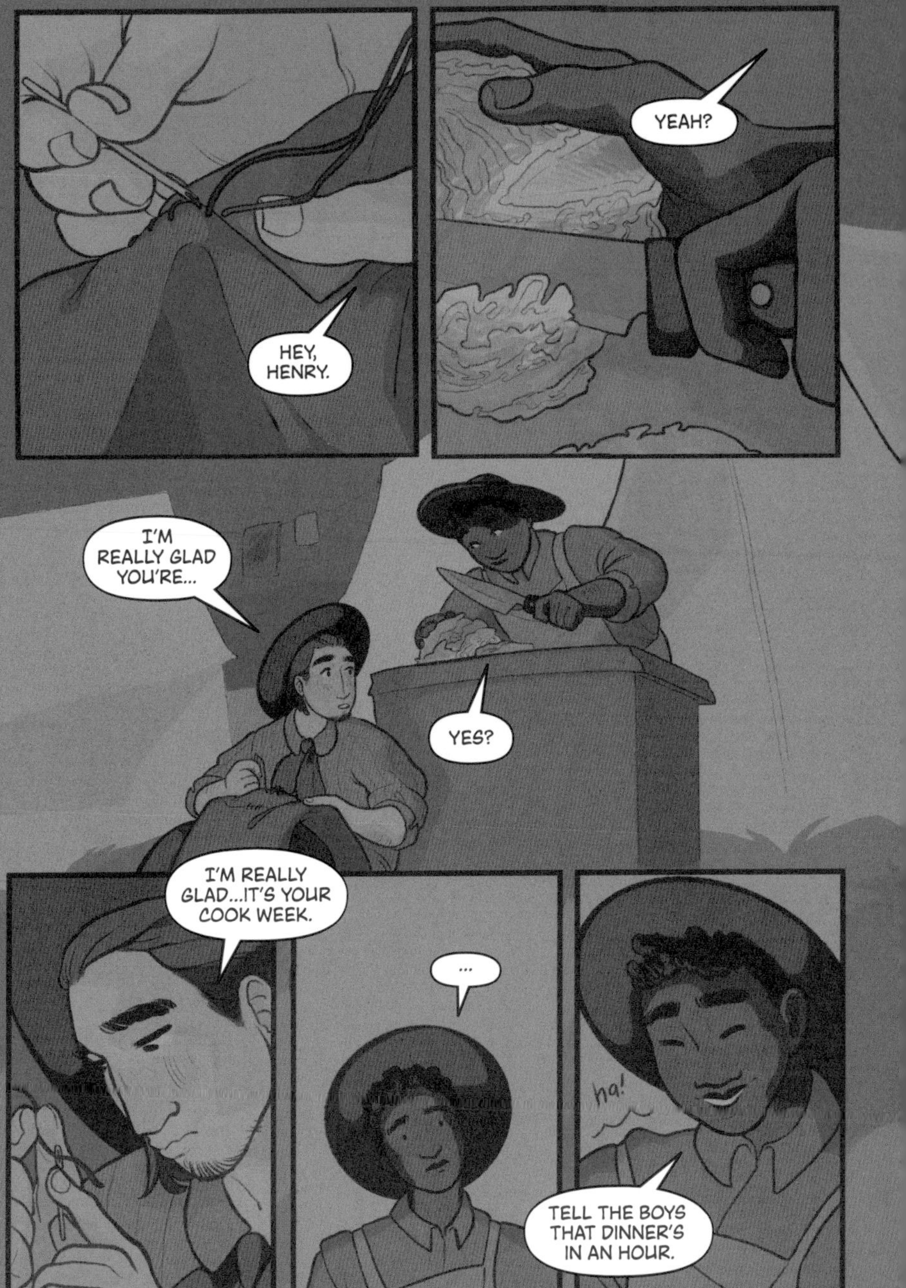
HEY, HENRY.
YEAH?
I'M REALLY GLAD YOU'RE...
YES?
I'M REALLY GLAD...IT'S YOUR COOK WEEK.
...
ha!
TELL THE BOYS THAT DINNER'S IN AN HOUR.

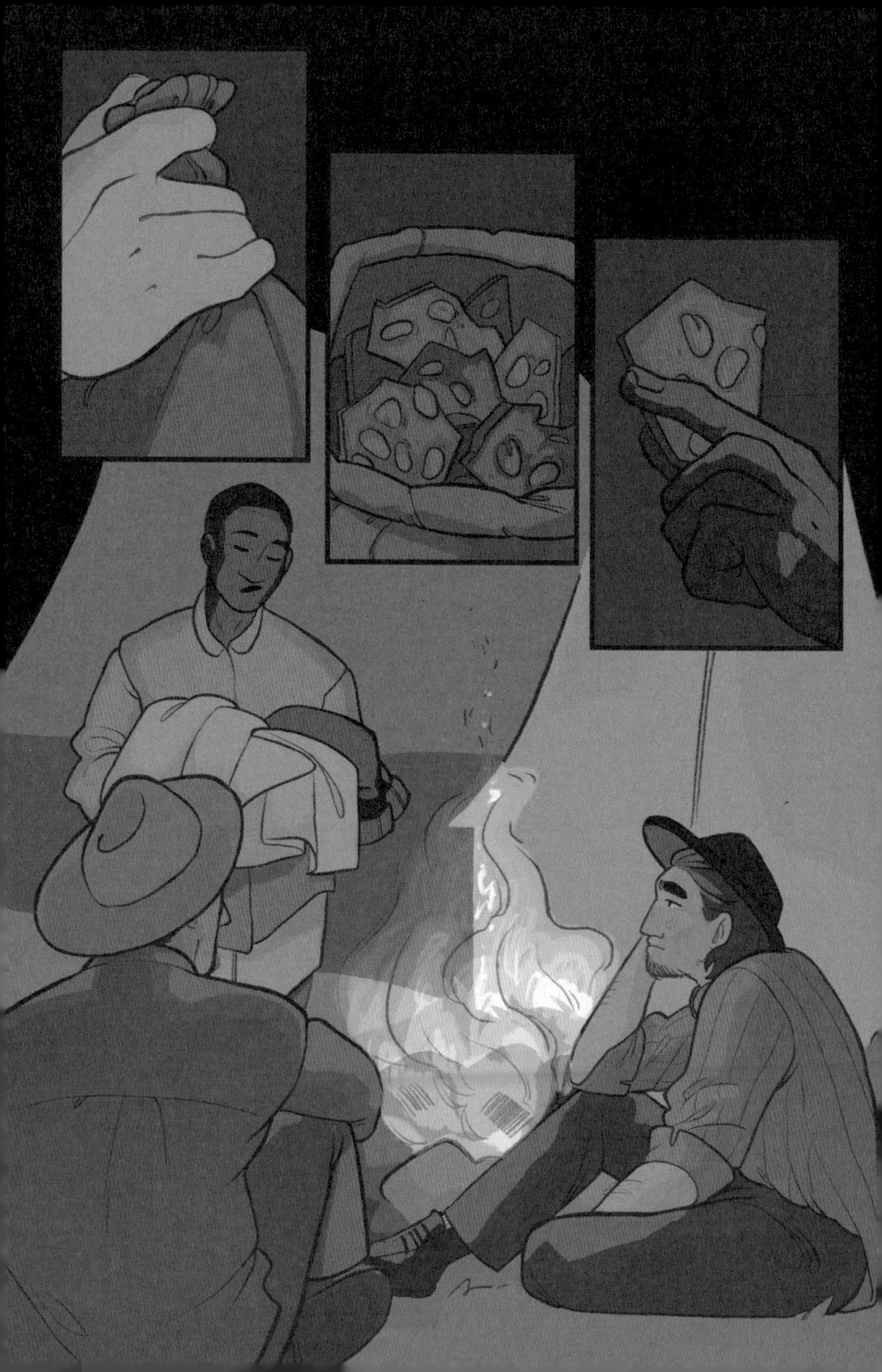

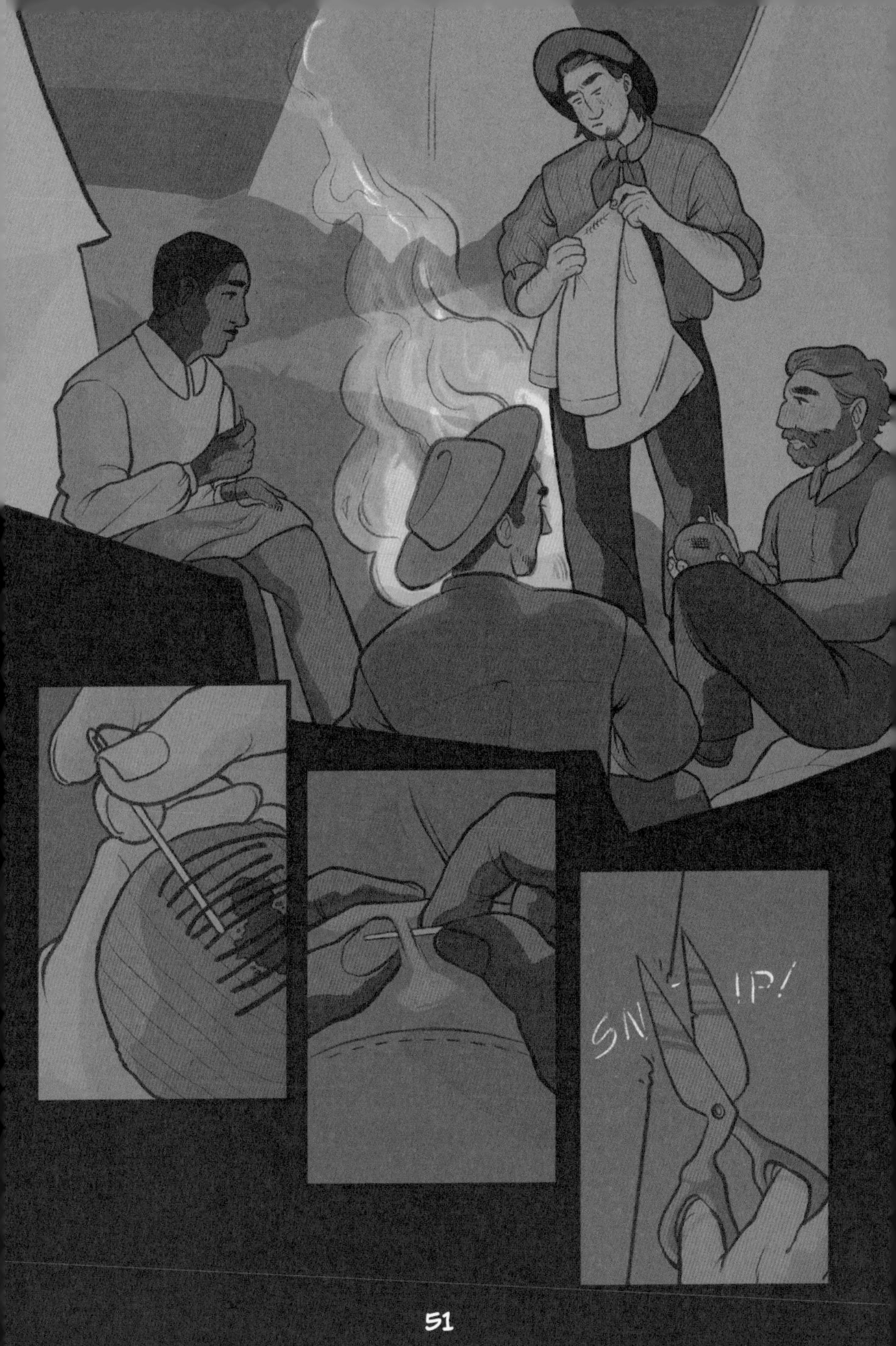
SN
IP!

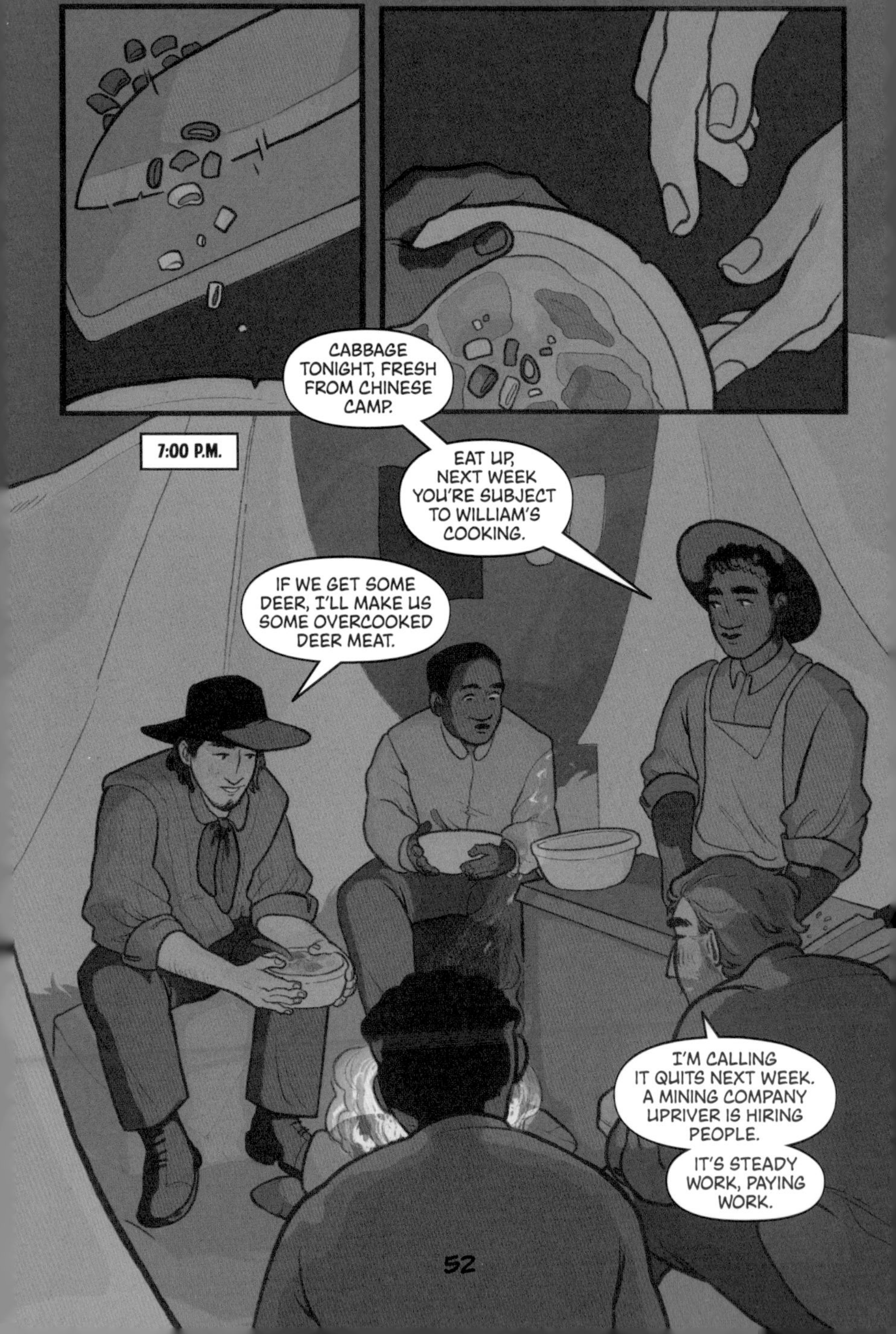
CABBAGE TONIGHT, FRESH FROM CHINESE CAMP.
7:00 P.M.
EAT UP, NEXT WEEK YOU'RE SUBJECT TO WILLIAM'S COOKING.
IF WE GET SOME DEER, I'LL MAKE US SOME OVERCOOKED DEER MEAT.
I'M CALLING IT QUITS NEXT WEEK. A MINING COMPANY UPRIVER IS HIRING PEOPLE.
IT'S STEADY WORK, PAYING WORK.

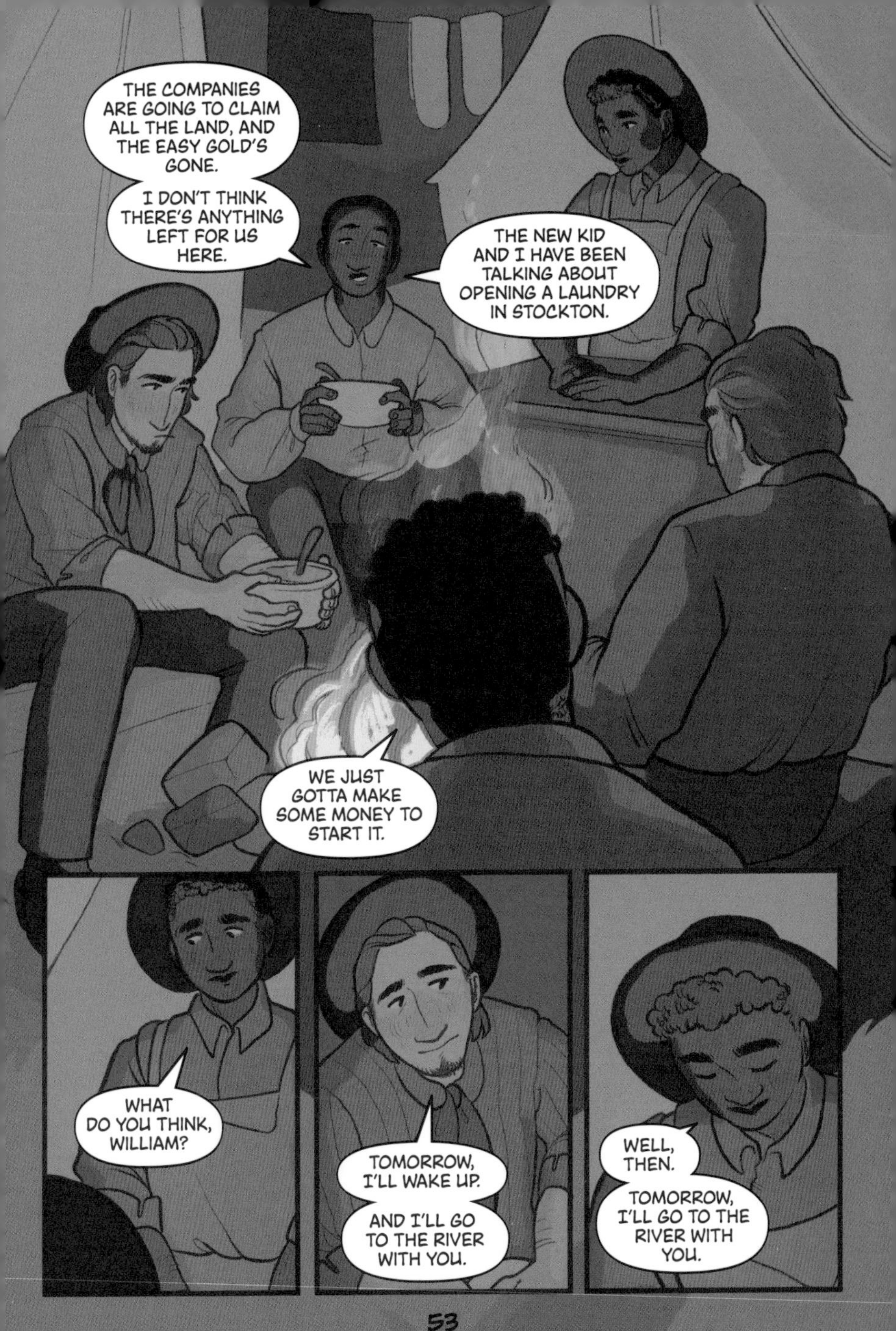
THE COMPANIES ARE GOING TO CLAIM ALL THE LAND, AND THE EASY GOLD'S GONE.
I DON'T THINK THERE'S ANYTHING LEFT FOR US HERE.
THE NEW KID AND I HAVE BEEN TALKING ABOUT OPENING A LAUNDRY IN STOCKTON.
WE JUST GOTTA MAKE SOME MONEY TO START IT.
WHAT DO YOU THINK, WILLIAM?
TOMORROW, I'LL WAKE UP.
AND I'LL GO TO THE RIVER WITH YOU.
WELL, THEN.
TOMORROW, I'LL GO TO THE RIVER WITH YOU.

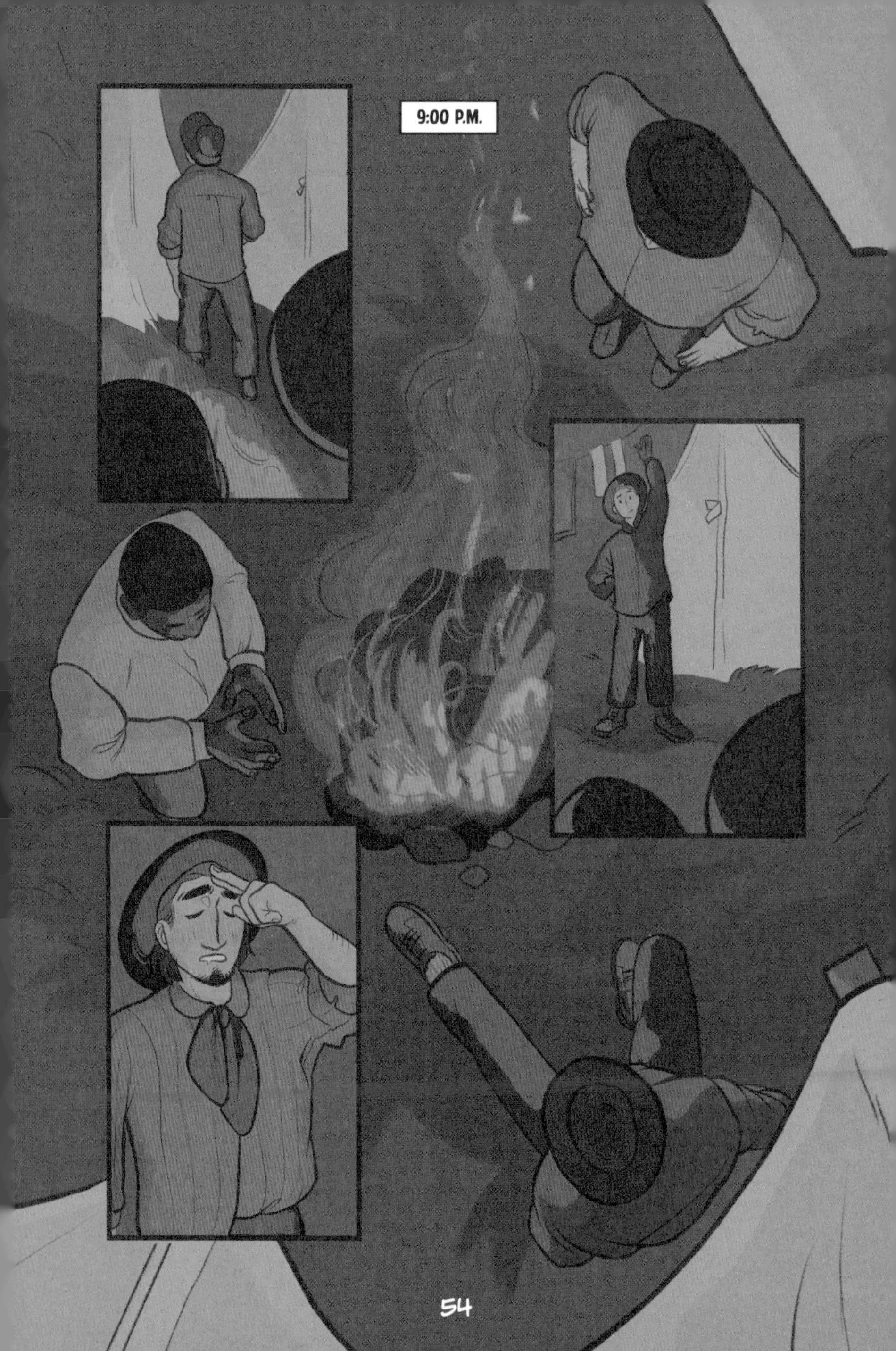
9:00 P.M.

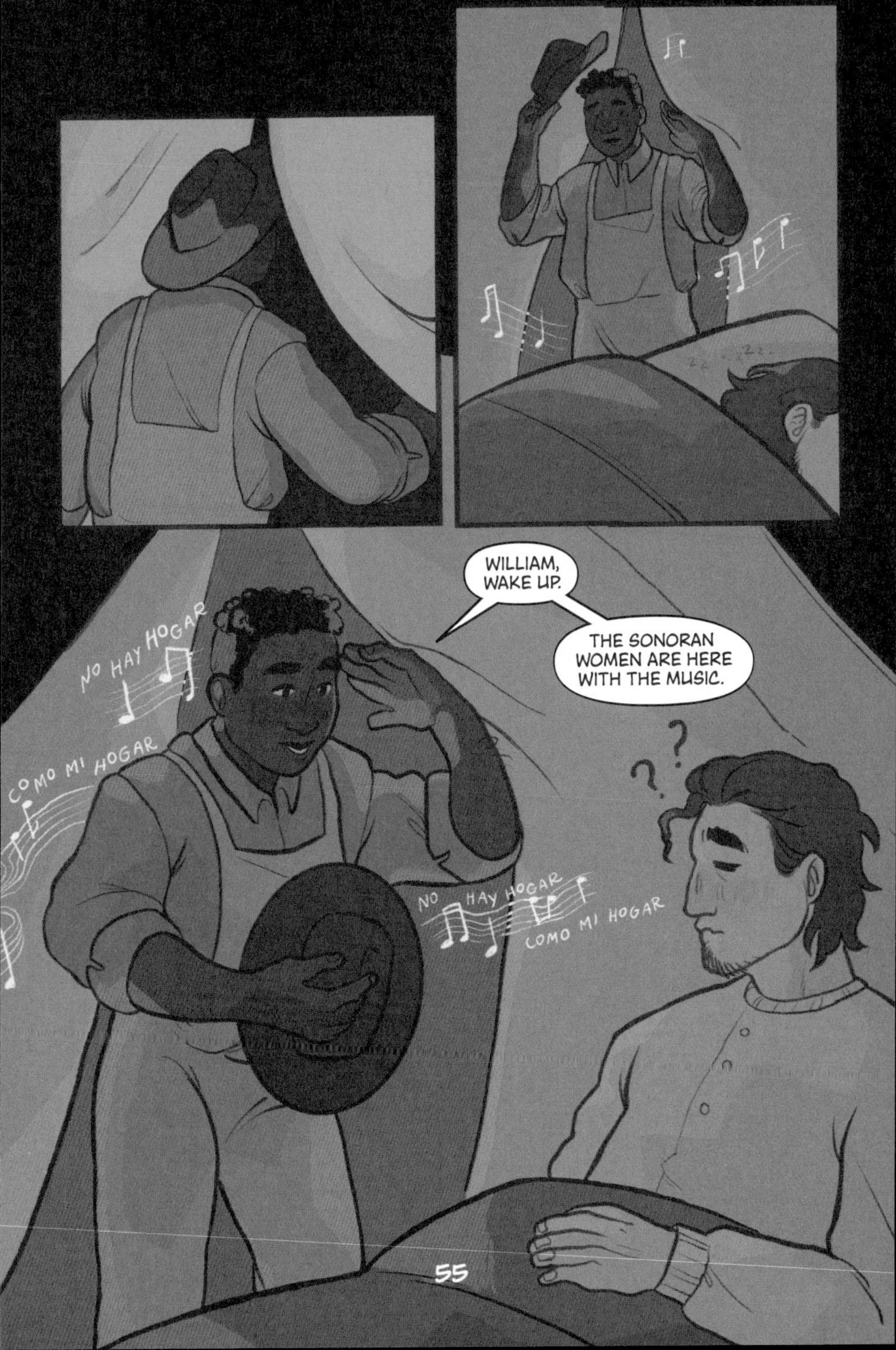
WILLIAM, WAKE UP.
THE SONORAN WOMEN ARE HERE WITH THE MUSIC.
NO HAY HOGAR
COMO MI HOGAR
NO HAY HOGAR
COMO MI HOGAR

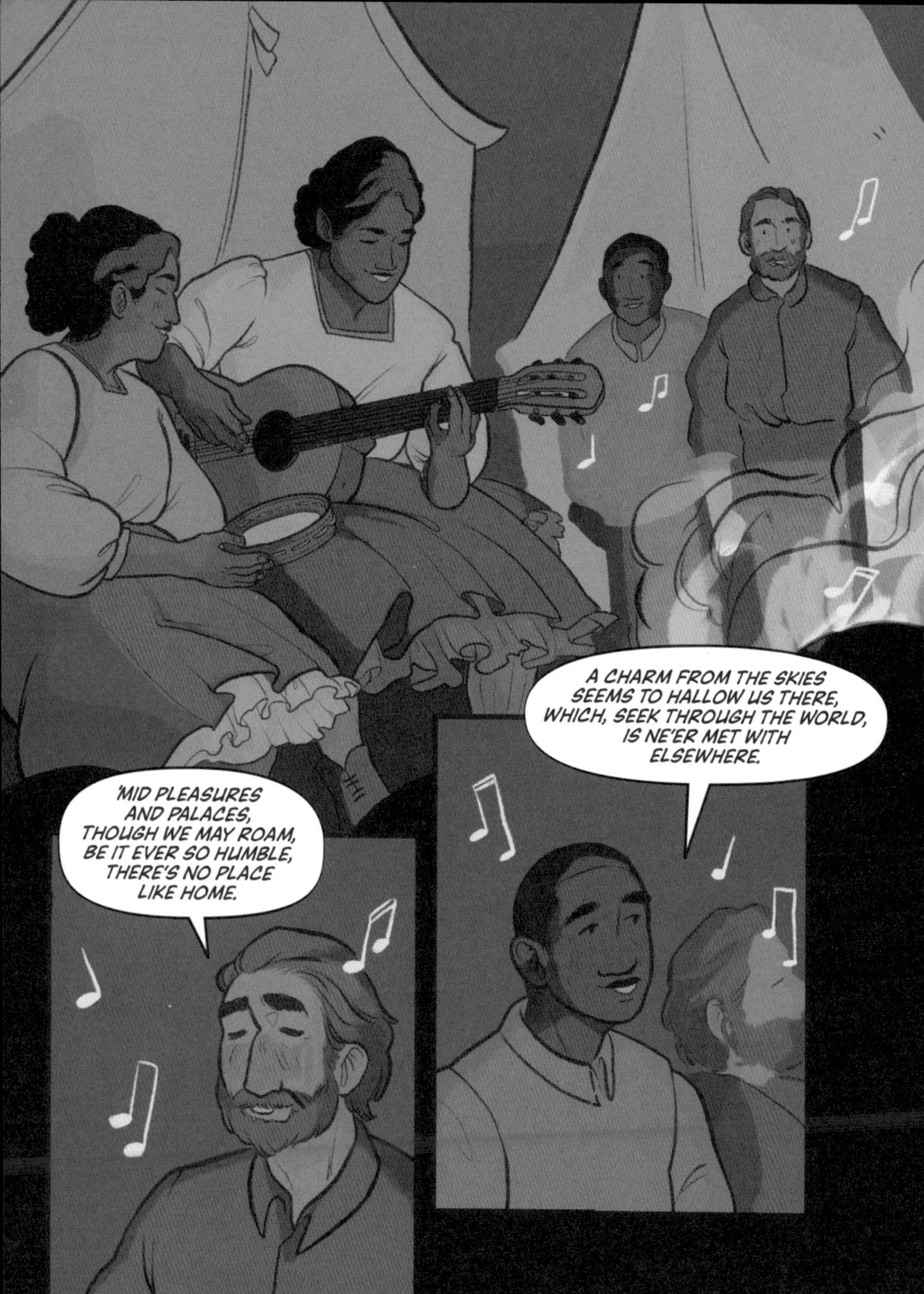

'MID PLEASURES AND PALACES, THOUGH WE MAY ROAM, BE IT EVER SO HUMBLE, THERE'S NO PLACE LIKE HOME.
A CHARM FROM THE SKIES SEEMS TO HALLOW US THERE, WHICH, SEEK THROUGH THE WORLD, IS NE'ER MET WITH ELSEWHERE.

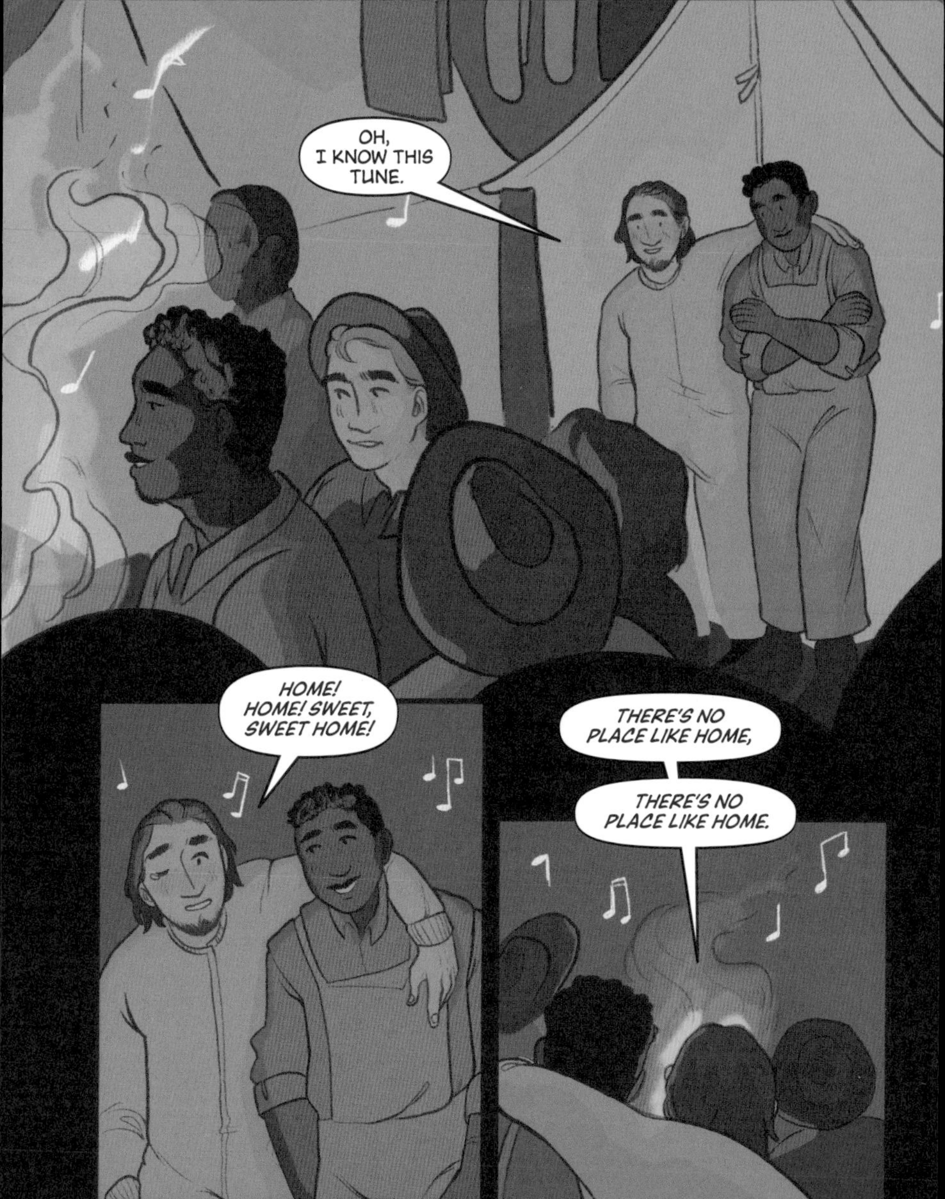
OH, I KNOW THIS TUNE.
HOME! HOME! SWEET, SWEET HOME!
THERE'S NO PLACE LIKE HOME,
THERE'S NO PLACE LIKE HOME.

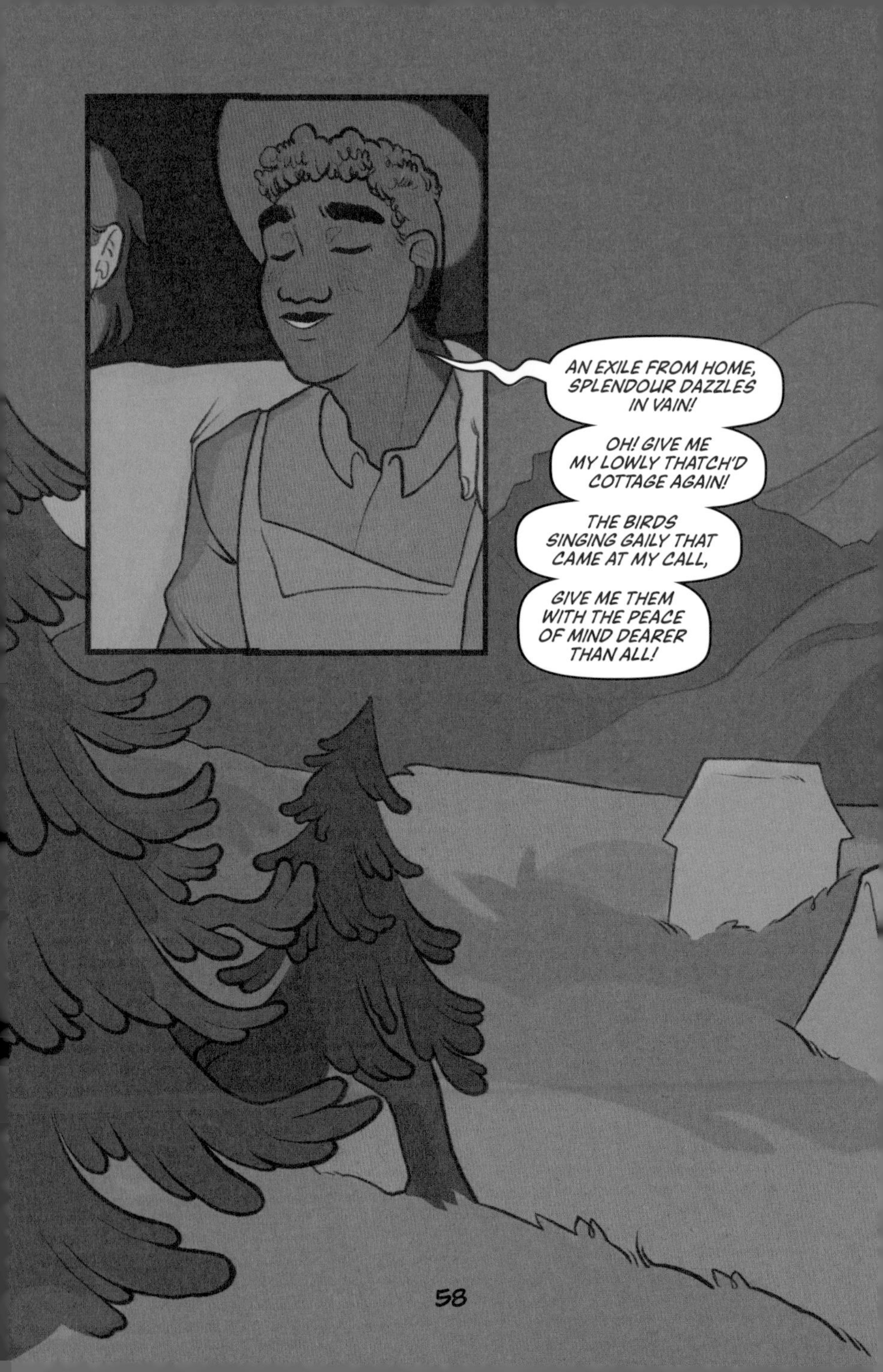
AN EXILE FROM HOME, SPLENDOUR DAZZLES IN VAIN!
OH! GIVE ME MY LOWLY THATCH'D COTTAGE AGAIN!
THE BIRDS SINGING GAILY THAT CAME AT MY CALL,
GIVE ME THEM WITH THE PEACE OF MIND DEARER THAN ALL!

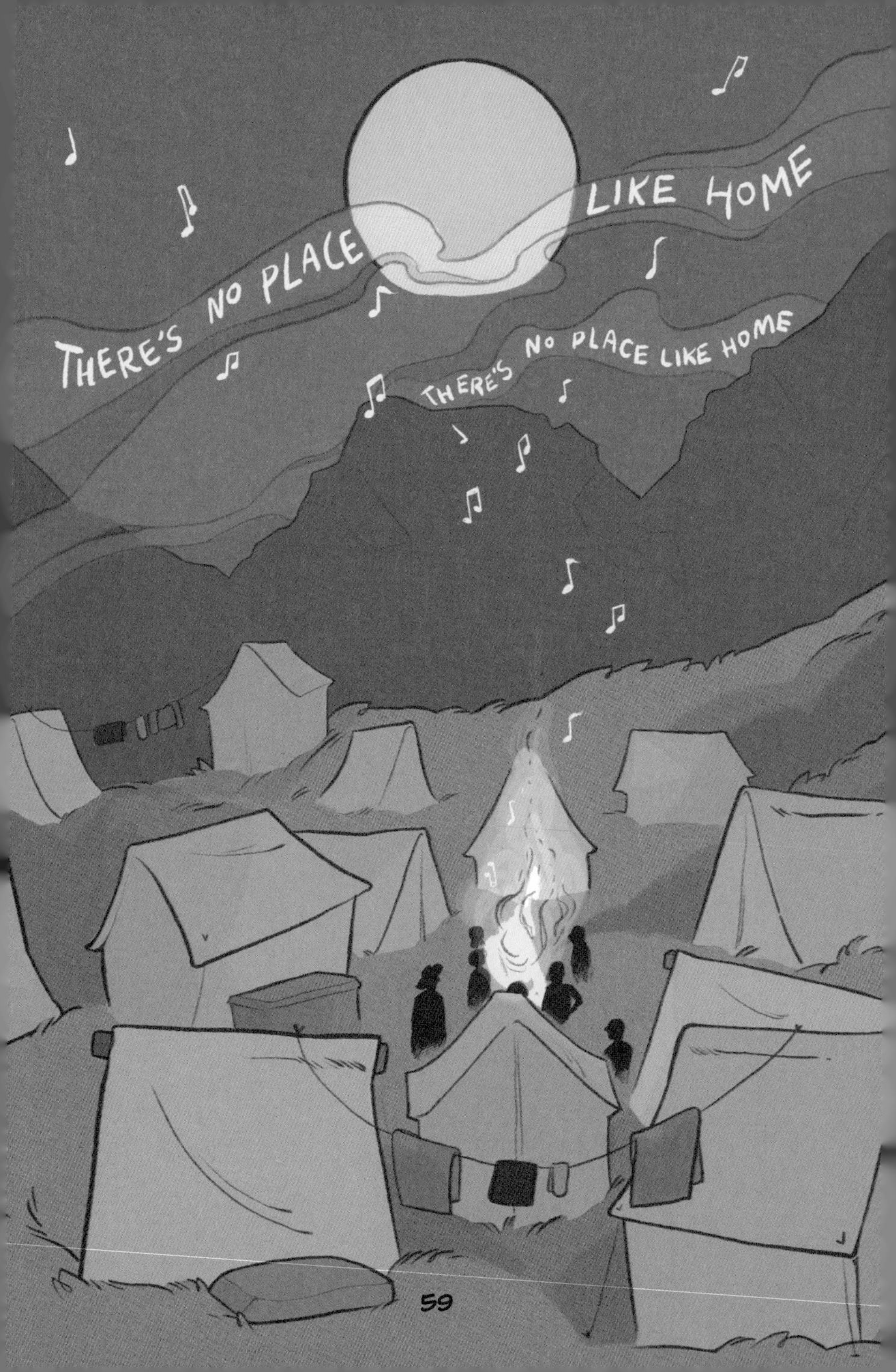

Conclusion

The Gold Rush is considered to have ended in 1855, when mining companies started building large-scale industrial equipment to retrieve the remaining gold. As a result, many independent miners were forced to find work with these companies or leave the goldfields for employment elsewhere.

The California Gold Rush changed the social and physical landscape of California forever. Immigrants from all over the country and world had flocked there, hopeful for new lives. Some returned to their homes disappointed. Others left the goldfields, but still settled down in California. In the span of just two years, San Francisco grew from a small town of one thousand people in 1848 to a thriving city of twenty-five thousand people in 1850. By 1870, there were one hundred and fifty thousand people in San Francisco!

The Gold Rush created a world where Chinese, Mexican, and European immigrants, Black and white Americans, and Indigenous people often worked in close proximity with one another, and as a result, created their own tight-knit communities as time went on.

However, this more diverse world was not without racism and conflict. For instance, the arrival of new cultures and people was devastating to the Indigenous population of California. The increase in population and in mining technology wrecked their natural landscape, while Indigenous people themselves experienced racism, enslavement, and mass murder by new settlers and the United States government.

Within ten years of joining the Union, California became known as the "Golden State." This nickname and reputation would continue to draw people from all over the world to California to chase their dreams of fame and fortune.

Timeline of the Gold Rush

1846 — California is part of Mexico

— San Francisco (then called Yerba Buena) has a population of two hundred

— California's Indigenous population is estimated at one hundred and fifty thousand

1848 — James Marshall discovers gold at John Sutter's sawmill

— The Treaty of Guadalupe Hidalgo is signed, ending the Mexican-American War and making California part of the United States

— The first newspaper article about the discovery of gold in California is published

1849 — Approximately ninety thousand people immigrate to California in search of gold

1850 — The first Foreign Miners' Tax Act is passed—protests from white immigrant miners quickly result in "free white persons" being excluded from the tax

— California becomes America's thirty-first state, entering the Union as a free state

1852 — California passes the state's Fugitive Slave Act

1855 — The Gold Rush ends—an estimated three hundred thousand people have arrived in California

1870 — California's Indigenous population is estimated at under thirty thousand

Bibliography

*Books for young readers

Akins, Damon B., and William J. Bauer Jr. *We Are the Land: A History of Native California*. Oakland, CA: University of California Press, 2021.

Brands, H. W. *The Age of Gold: The California Gold Rush and the New American Dream*. New York: Doubleday, 2002.

Chang, Iris. *The Chinese in America: A Narrative History*. New York: Penguin Books, 2004.

Dolnick, Edward. *The Rush: America's Fevered Quest for Fortune, 1848-1853*. New York: Little, Brown and Company, 2014.

*Holub, Joan. *What Was the Gold Rush?* New York: Penguin Workshop, 2013.

Johnson, Susan Lee. *Roaring Camp: The Social World of the California Gold Rush*. New York: W. W. Norton & Company, 2000.

Parins, James W. *John Rollin Ridge: His Life and Works*. Lincoln, NE: University of Nebraska Press, 2004.

ABOUT THE CREATORS

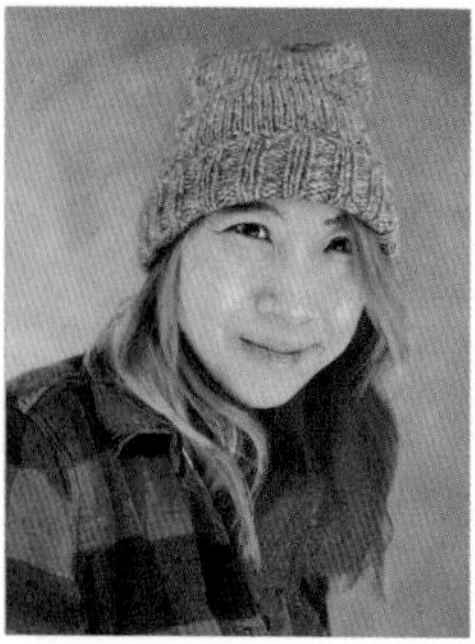

Shing Yin Khor is the author of *The Legend of Auntie Po*, a National Book Award finalist about a young logging-camp cook in the Sierra Nevada telling Paul Bunyan tales, and of *The American Dream?*, a graphic novel memoir about driving Route 66. They tell stories about nostalgic Americana, immigration, and new rituals. They live in Los Angeles with a small dog and a cargo van.

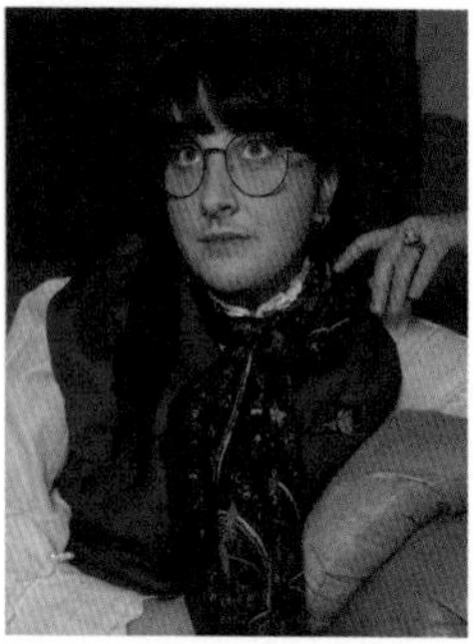

Kass Gray is a freelance illustrator, cartoonist, and recent graduate from the Columbus College of Art and Design. He currently resides in Columbus, Ohio, with a very large cat called Cicero (and his human roommates). He has always had a particular penchant for history in all its forms, and loves to tell stories that capture the forgotten or seldom told lives of the past.